Blender 3.0

The beginner's guide

D1709985

Allan Brito

Description and data

Technical info about the book

Author: Allan Brito

Edition: 1st

Cover image credits: Li Zhang @Unsplash - Licensed in public domain - https://unsplash.com/license

Blender version used in the Book: *3.0*

ISBN: 9798401860637

First edition date: January 2022

Imprint: Independently published

Editing and design: Allan Brito

Help and support:

https://www.blender3darchitect.com/contact/

About the author

Allan Brito is a Brazilian architect that has a passion for applying technology and open source to design and visualization. He is a longtime Blender user, staring with Blender 2.3x back in 2005. One of his goals is to help artists using Blender in the architecture and visual design fields.

You will find more about him and the use of Blender for architecture and design in **blender3darchitect.com**, where he writes articles about the subject daily.

Who should read this book?

The primary objective of this book is to give any aspiring or experienced digital artist a fast way to start using Blender 3.0 with confidence. From simple concepts like user interface manipulation to more advanced topics such as light and rendering. We will start from the very beginning, covering critical steps required to get you comfortable with Blender. If you are planning to create 3D models, animations, and overall rendering, this book will help you start from scratch.

By the end of this book, you will have a solid knowledge of how Blender 3.0 works and what it takes to create digital content.

You don't need any previous experience with Blender to follow the chapters.

Foreword

The release of version 2.8, back in 2018, was a massive milestone for Blender and brought a lot of attention to the software as a reliable and accessible platform to create digital content. With a revamped user interface and the adoption of simple standards from other graphical applications, you can easily state that it was a game-changer for many artists and companies.

In Blender 3.0, you find a consolidation of this evolution from the past years with a more polished user experience and cutting-edge technologies. We have an impressive Asset Browser for fast reuse of assets and lots of improvements in the rendering field, with both Eevee and Cycles getting optimizations from the list of new features.

Nowadays, Blender is an essential player in several industries with support from multiple companies like Apple, NVIDIA, AMD, Epic Games, Intel, Ubisoft, Google, and even Microsoft. All of them contribute to the development of Blender.

Our purpose with *The Beginner's Guide* for Blender 3.0 is to explain how Blender works from the perspective of an inexperienced artist or someone who wants to become a digital artist.

We start with the user interface basics and move to other topics such as 3D modeling, rendering, and animation. Even if you are trying to migrate from older versions of Blender, the guide will also be helpful.

I hope you enjoy the content, and by the end of the book, you feel more comfortable using Blender for all your projects!

Allan Brito

Downloading Blender

One of the most significant advantages of Blender when comparing to similar tools is their open-source nature. You can use Blender without any hidden costs or subscriptions! All you have to do is download Blender and start using it. How to download? To download Blender, you should visit the *Blender Foundation* website:

```
https://www.blender.org/download/
```

Another option is to get a development version, which has the most up to date tools and features:

```
https://builder.blender.org
```

The development versions offer a peek of upcoming releases as *alpha* and *beta* versions. They feature new tools and options, but may also have bugs and instabilities. You should not use them for critical projects. For this book, we will use version *3.0 of Blender*, but the vast majority of techniques will still work with later versions.

Using the following address gives you access to the entire release history of Blender:

```
https://download.blender.org/release/
```

In the release history, it is possible to get current and old versions of Blender. For instance, you can download Blender 1.0! What version should you download? Get the latest stable release from the Blender Foundation website; it is the safest option. Use the first link from this section.

Download book files

You can download the Blender files used in the book in the following address:

```
https://www.blender3darchitect.com/b30beginners
```

All files use Blender 2.83, 2.9, or 3.0. The ZIP file will include:

– Base files

– Textures

– HDR maps

– 3D Models

Intentionally left blank

TABLE OF CONTENTS

Chapter 1 - Blender user interface and 3D navigation

The first chapter of our guide for Blender 3.0 focuses on core concepts regarding user interface, 3D navigation, shortcuts, and the overall use of Blender. For instance, you learn how to handle object selection with both keyboard shortcuts and the mouse.

Only after learning those basic concepts can we move to more intermediate and advanced topics in the book. If you are new to Blender, you should not skip this chapter. Read and practice with each topic until you are comfortable going around both 3D space and user interface.

Here is a list of what you will learn:

– Handling object selection and navigation

– Working with the user interface

– Choosing and changing editors

– Using keyboard shortcuts and Editors

– Working with 3D Cursor and the Snap tool

– Moving and placing objects based on the 3D Cursor location

1.1 First time with Blender

After installing Blender on your computer, you will open the software and see a quick setup screen that will ask a few questions. The most crucial choice you have to make on this screen is how you want to handle object selection. The screen only appears when opening Blender for the first time.

In the past, Blender used the *right mouse button* to select objects, which is the opposite of all other graphical applications. Starting back in Blender 2.8, the new default behavior uses the *left mouse button* for selection.

You can confirm in the *Quick Setup* the *left button* for selection and keep all other options in their default settings. Unless you have a particular need to change those settings, leave all options in their default values.

For the rest of the book, I will assume you choose the "Left" option (*Select With*) from the Quick Setup (Figure 1.1).

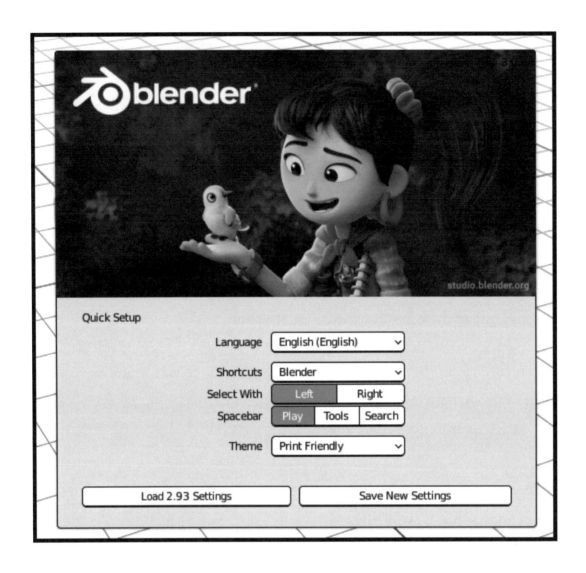

Figure 1.1 - *Blender Quick Setup*

You can always change those settings later in Blender using the **Edit → Preferences...** menu. To modify your selection button, use the Keymap tab in the preferences, which will allow you to swap between the left or right mouse buttons for selection (Figure 1.2).

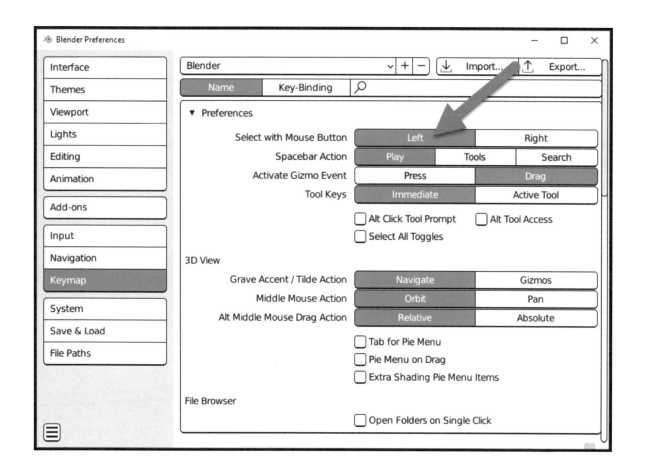

Figure 1.2 - *User preferences*

Why is that so important? Because some additional options regarding the user interface work based on the current selection button. For instance, if you choose the *right-button* for selection, we won't have the context menu.

After setting all options with the Quick Setup, you will see the Blender user interface. At first, it may look intimidating for artists coming from other graphical applications, but with practice, you will start to become familiar with the structure.

Info: At the Quick Setup, you will also have an option to pick a theme for your Blender User Interface. The default theme is "Blender Dark." For the book, I will use "Print Friendly" to make sure you have a better view of all screenshots. You can change the theme at any time using the Edit → Preferences... menu and go to the Theme tab.

In Figure 1.3, you can see the default user interface of Blender.

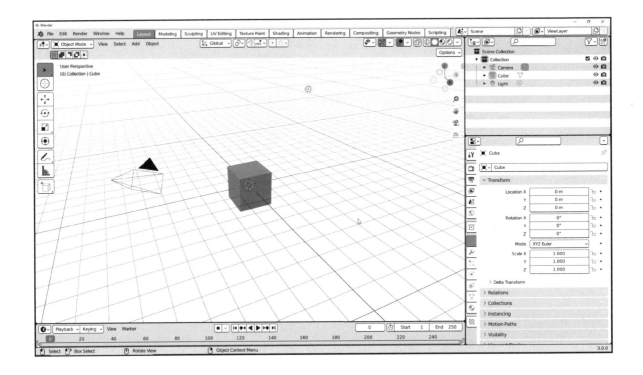

Figure 1.3 - Default user interface

That is the default user interface because it is what you see every time Blender starts after a fresh install. You can rearrange and modify Editors from the interface in several ways. What is an Editor? Each division in the interface is an Editor that has the purpose of handling a particular type of data.

For instance, you will find the large space at the center with a single cube, camera, and light as the 3D Viewport. That is the Editor responsible for displaying 3D data and will also allow you to manipulate 3D models. There you can work with 3D modeling and visualize your projects in a tridimensional space.

Other essential Editors in Blender:

- **Properties Editor**: Shows options regarding the selected object to edit and change properties like materials, modifiers, and more.

- **Outliner**: List all objects in a scene and also give access to collections of objects. You can also rename and control the visualization of objects.

- **Timeline**: Give you a quick way to control animation data to add and set frames and keyframes.

In each Editor header, you will find a selector that lists all other types of available Editors. By clicking at the selector, you can swap the current Editor with any other from the list (Figure 1.4).

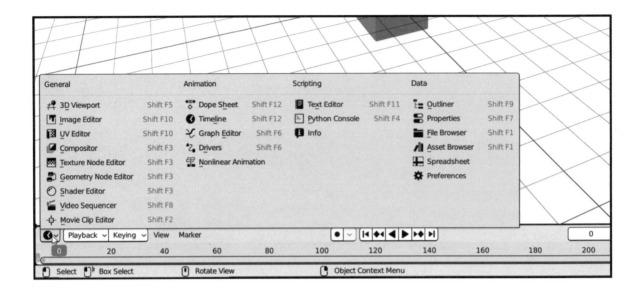

Figure 1.4 - *Editor selector*

That is useful when you want to quickly access tools available at a particular Editor in Blender without the need to create new interface divisions.

Tip: Every Editor has a horizontal header that displays additional menus and options. It is usually at the top of each Editor. By right-clicking at the header, you can flip their position either to the top or bottom.

1.1.1 Splitting and managing editors

As a way to customize the user interface for your needs, you can resize and modify the divisions for each Editor. To resize an Editor, place your mouse cursor at the border of an Editor. Once the cursor turns to a double arrow, you can click and drag to resize (Figure 1.5).

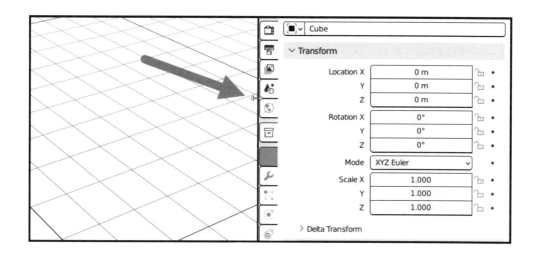

Figure 1.5 - *Double arrow cursor*

If you want to make divisions or join two Editors, you will have to right-click at the border of an existing editor. Once you right-click, you will see the Area Options menu (Figure 1.6).

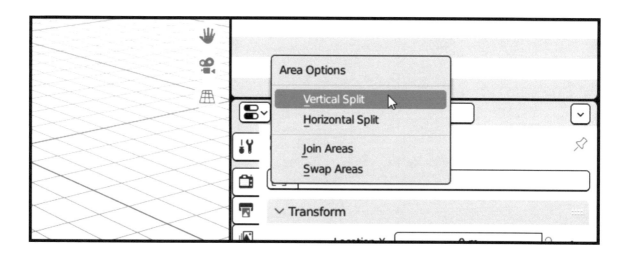

Figure 1.6 - *Area Options*

There you will find:

- **Vertical Split**: Creates a vertical division at your current Editor.

- **Horizontal Split**: Creates a horizontal division at your current Editor.- **Join Areas**: Join two editors that share the same border.

- **Swap Areas**: Here, you can swap between the two Editors sharing the border where you right-clicked.

To join two editors in the interface, they must share the same border. Once you start the joining process, your mouse cursor turns into a small arrow, which will allow you to choose which Editor expands (Figure 1.7).

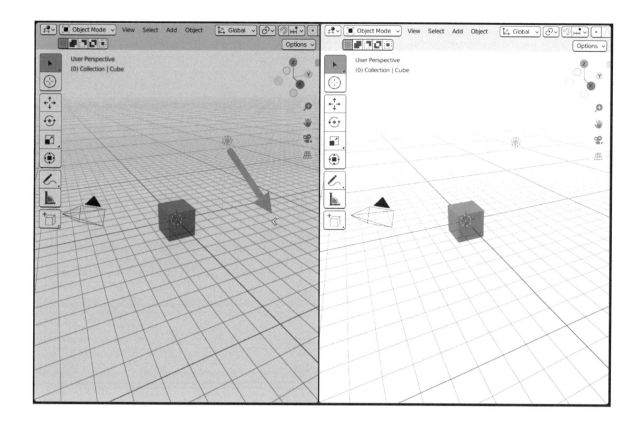

Figure 1.7 - *Expansion arrow*

Knowing how to handle Editors and divisions is essential to keep you productive in Blender.

Tip: You can also use the **View** → **Area** → **Duplicate Area into New Window** *to detach an Editor from the interface. That is useful to move Editors between multiple monitors.*

1.1.2 Using WorkSpaces

At some point in your work using Blender, you will have a user interface arrangement that helps in a particular task. It is possible to reuse that interface layout in other projects. In Blender, we have a tool called WorkSpaces, a set of predefined Editors you can activate at any time.

There are several pre-made WorkSpaces available in Blender that you can choose using the selector at the top of your 3D Viewport (Figure 1.8).

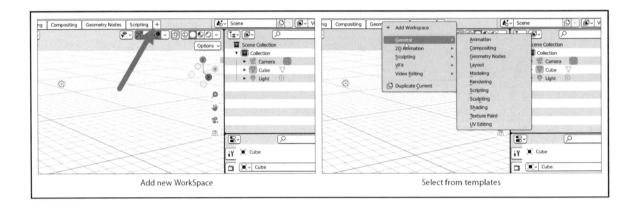

Figure 1.8 - WorkSpace selector

You find WorkSpaces optimized for tasks like modeling, animation, and video editing. WorkSpaces are only an interface arrangement and won't have any effect on 3D data.

How to save an existing interface as a new WorkSpace? You can easily keep an existing layout as a new WorkSpace by clicking at the "+" icon at the top of your 3D Viewport and choosing "Duplicate Current." That will create a new tab at the top of your interface. You can double-click the tab to assign a unique name to that Work-Space.

To remove a WorkSpace from your user interface, you can *right-click* at the Work-Space name and choose the "Delete" option (Figure 1.9).

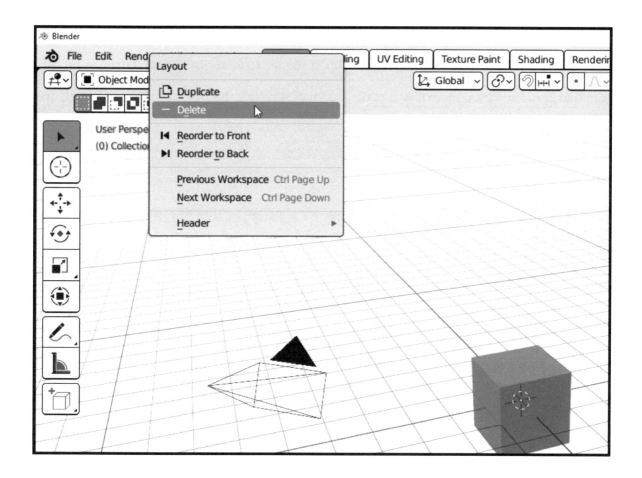

Figure 1.9 - *New WorkSpace*

Tip: *You can also rearrange the WorkSpace order at the top of your 3D Viewport by clicking and dragging the tabs.*

1.2 Saving files and reusing content

After a few minutes or hours working on a project using Blender, you will most likely want to save your progress. To save a file in Blender, use the **File → Save As...** menu, where you will be able to pick a folder to save your project file. The format Blender uses has an extension of ".blend" and will be your container for all information regarding your project.

In some cases, you will also see additional files in your folder with extensions like ".blend1", which are backup copies from your projects that Blender automatically creates.

One of the benefits of saving a project in Blender, besides avoid losing your data, is the possibility of reusing some of your content. From 3D models to WorkSpaces, you can pull almost all data from a Blender file to later projects.

For instance, if you made a useful WorkSpace that you want to reuse in a new project. You can quickly get that WorkSpace using the *Append* or *Link* options from the File menu (Figure 1.10).

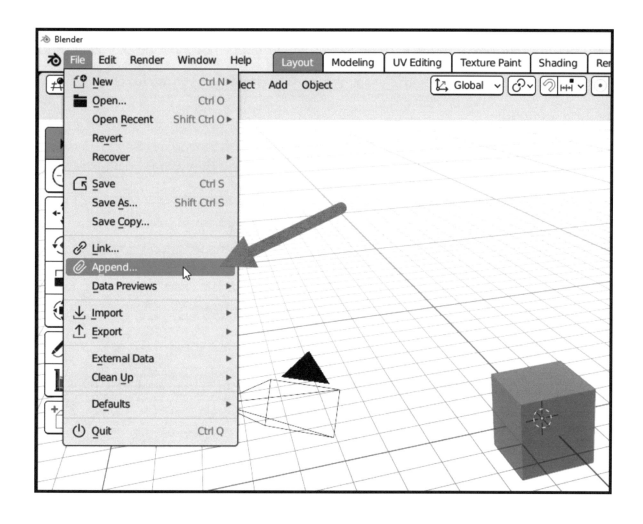

Figure 1.10 - *Append and Link*

The Append option incorporates data into a new file, which merges the information to your current project. The Link option creates a relative connection to the original project file saved. It means the data won't stay at your current project, but in the external Blender file, from where you pulled the asset.

If you want to make changes to the asset, like a material or 3D model, you should pick the Append option. For the cases where you don't need to make changes, use the Link option.

For instance, if you want to get a WorkSpace from another Blender file saved in your hard drive, go to the **File** → **Append** menu and locate the file. Once you click at the filename, you will see a list of folders (Figure 1.11).

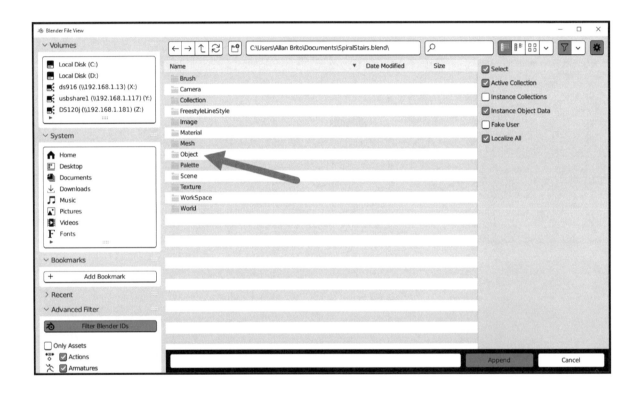

Figure 1.11 - Folders for Append

Each folder has a type of data you can pull from the file. One of them has the name of WorkSpace, and inside, you will see a list of all your existing WorkSpaces for that file. Select the WorkSpace you want and press the "Append from Library" button (Figure 1.12).

Figure 1.12 - WorkSpaces in folder

After appending the data, you will see the WorkSpace in your user interface. The same process applies to all other assets you want to bring from external files. You can use the Append option to pull 3D models, materials, textures, animation, or anything else you wish to reuse.

Info: As you might see from the example of the Append tool, it is imperative to assign meaningful names inside Blender. Whenever you have an object that you want to use later in future projects, it will make the process a lot easier to locate important assets by name.

1.3 Active editor and shortcuts

Before we start to discuss shortcuts and tools for 3D navigation in Blender, you must become familiar with a core concept of the user interface. You must be aware of the active Editor. The active Editor is vital to define where you will use a particular shortcut or tool in Blender.

What is the active Editor? That is the Editor in which you have the mouse cursor located by the time you trigger a shortcut.

That is important because sometimes you will use a particular shortcut for a task, and you only want to update data from a particular Editor. For instance, you might want to erase a keyframe inside an Editor called Timeline. You must place the mouse cursor above the Timeline Editor to erase data in that Editor.

To erase anything in Blender, you can either press the X key or DELETE. Both shortcuts will erase data like 3D models and keyframes. If you have a 3D model selected and also a keyframe in the Timeline, and press the DELETE key. What will Blender erase?

If you have the mouse cursor above the 3D Viewport, the 3D model will vanish from your project. To erase the keyframe, you must press the key when the mouse cursor is above the Timeline.

The concept of an active Editor is essential for all shortcuts in Blender. With the active Editor, you can choose where to apply a keyboard shortcut.

1.4 3D Navigation and zoom controls

The 3D Viewport is the most important Editor in the Blender user interface regarding modeling and visualization of your 3D data. In this Editor, we can also use several tools and shortcuts to successfully navigate the 3D space. Blender uses a combination of mouse and keyboard shortcuts to navigate in 3D.

Here is a list with the most common shortcuts for 3D Navigation:

- **Middle mouse button**: Press and hold the button and move the cursor to start rotating your view.

- **SHIFT+ Middle mouse button**: Press the keys and drag your mouse to move your screen (Pan).

- **CTRL+Middle mouse button**: Press both keys and move your mouse up and down for zoom in and out.

- **Numpad 5**: Swap between orthographic and perspective projections.

– **Numpad 1**: Front view

– **Numpad 3**: Right view

– **Numpad 7**: Top view

– **Home key**: Zoom all objects in your scene

If you press the CTRL key alongside each one of the Numpad 1, 3, and 7, you will get the opposite view. For instance, you will get the Left View by pressing the CTRL+Numpad 3.

An easy and fast way to navigate in 3D involves the backquote key from your keyboard. After pressing the ` key, a pie menu appears will multiple options to change your current view (Figure 1.13).

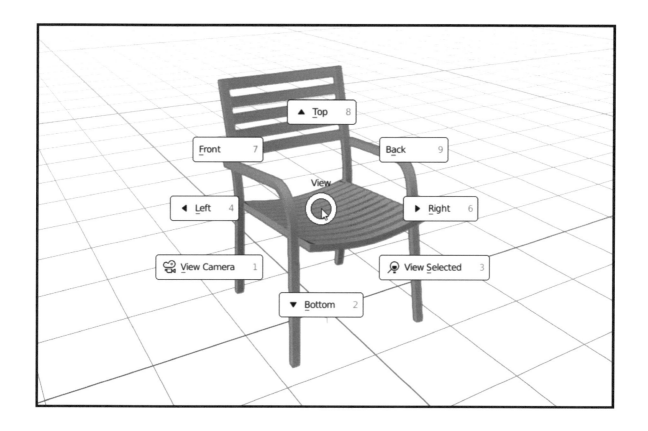

Figure 1.13 - *Pie Menu with view options*

That pie menu shows options with all orthographic views and a couple more. For instance, it is possible to jump straight into the active camera view or "View Selected." By choosing this last option makes your 3D Viewport to zoom in and focus on any selected objects.

With the backquote shortcut, you have a quick way to navigate without the need for numeric keyboard entry. However, a numeric keyboard (*Numpad*) still is an essential tool to navigate in 3D using Blender quickly. For instance, using the

Numpad 5 is the quickest way to swap between a perspective and orthographic projection.

What if you don't have a keyboard with a Numpad? You can emulate the Numpad functions using the **Edit** → **Preferences...** menu and going to the Input tab (Figure 1.14).

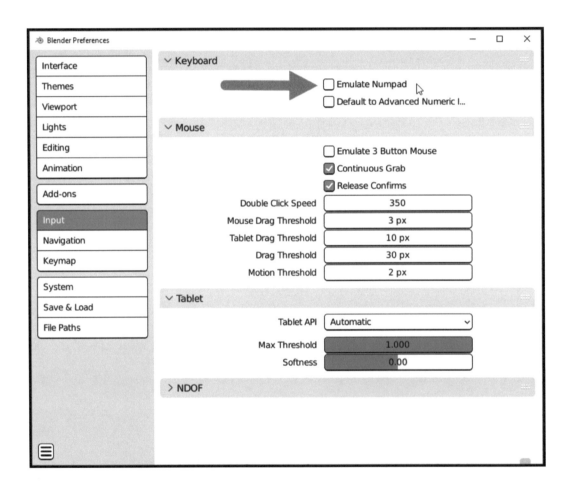

Figure 1.14 - Emulate Numpad

There you will find an option to emulate the Numpad. Enable the option, and you will have the alphanumeric keys working as if they were the numeric keyboard.

Besides those shortcuts, you also have navigation buttons on the top right of your 3D Viewport. They will help you with a mouse, only 3D navigation (Figure 1.15).

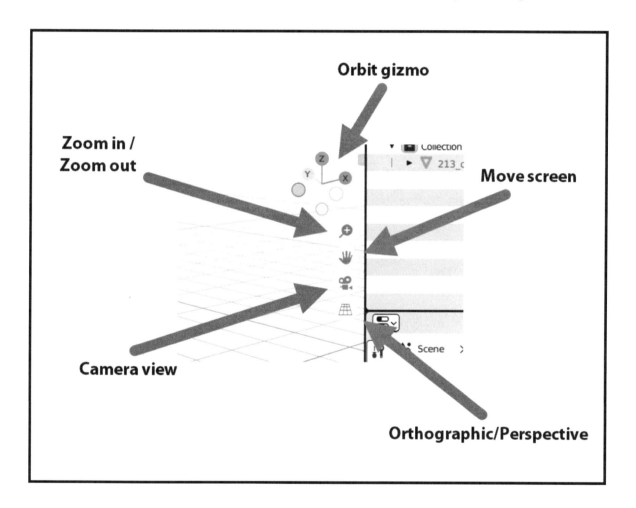

Figure 1.15 - *Navigation buttons*

The navigation buttons have similar options to the shortcuts with mouse and keyboard. For instance, if you want a more interactive way to go around in the 3D space, you can use the Orbit gizmo.

By clicking and dragging with the mouse inside the Gizmo, you will be able to rotate your view. Using the circles inside the Gizmo also activates orthographic views for your scene. For instance, using the circle with a Z inside makes your view jump to the top.

Info: All navigation and zoom controls will work on most of the Editor in Blender. Unless they don't have compatible data. For instance, you will only be able to use 3D rotation in the Viewport.

1.5 Object selection

Assuming you choose the *left mouse button* for selection in the Quick Setup menu, you will use that button for all selection tasks in Blender. No matter if you are in the 3D Viewport or any other Editor, your selection options and shortcuts remain the same.

If you want to select an object or feature in Blender, click on it regardless of the Editor. For selections of multiple instances in Blender, use the SHIFT key. Hold the SHIFT key and left-click at multiple objects, to either include or remove them from a selection.

Info: From this point forward, I will assume you choose the left button for selection. Whenever I mention a selection, you will perform it using a left-click.

You will see an orange outline highlighting all selected objects (Figure 1.16).

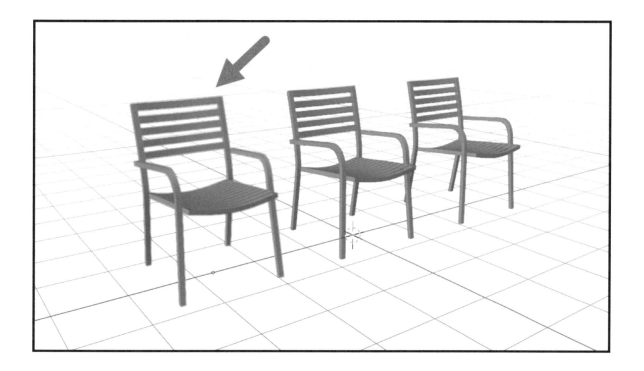

Figure 1.16 - *Outline in multiple objects*

From that outline, you will also notice that your last selected object has a brighter color for the outline. In Blender, you have something called an active object. That will be the last object you add to a selection.

Having control over your active object in a selection using multiple objects is important sometimes because you need to use that active object. For instance, in animation projects, you can create parenting relations to objects. When you create a parenting relation between objects, your active object will always be the dominant object.

It is possible to make any object from a selection to become active. After selecting multiple objects, hold the SHIFT key, and click at any of the selected objects. That object will become active.

How to remove an object from a selection? You must hold the SHIFT key and double-click at any object. The first click makes the object active, and the second removes it from the selection. If you are trying to remove the active object from selection, one click will be enough.

Here is a summary of your selection shortcuts:

– **SHIFT+Left-Click**: Add objects to the selection

– **SHIFT+Left-Click (with selected objects)**: Turn the object active in the selection

– **SHIFT+Left-Click (In the active object)**: Remove it from the selection

– **SHIFT+Left-Click twice (Any object but the active)**: Remove an object from the selection

As you can see from the list, you will handle most of the selections using the Left-Click and the SHIFT key. There are also some important shortcuts for object selection:

- **B key**: Makes a box selection, which draws a rectangular shape in your interface. All objects in the box area will be selected. If you hold the SHIFT key while drawing the box, you will remove the objects from the selection.

- **A key**: Add all objects to the selection if you don't have anything selected.

- **ALT+A**: Removes all objects from a selection.

- **CTRL+I**: Invert the selection, which is a great way to get multiple objects selected and leave just a few unselected.

Besides selection shortcuts, you will also find a few options to select objects in the 3D Viewport Toolbar (Figure 1.17).

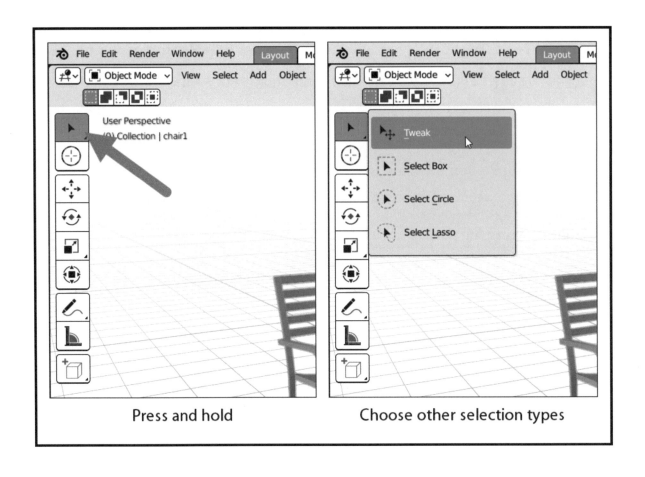

Figure 1.17 - *Toolbar options*

If you click and hold the "Select Box" icon, you will expand the button to display all options related selection.

With the select circle, you will be able to "paint" a selection by click and dragging the small circle that will appear on your screen. The lasso enables you to draw a shape that adds all objects inside to the selection.

Info: *A significant aspect of the selection shortcuts is that you can use them in all editors. The same keys work regardless of the Editor you have at the moment.*

1.6 The 3D Cursor

A core element of the Blender user interface is the 3D Cursor, which is that small crosshair icon that you will see in the 3D Viewport. The Cursor has an essential role in the use of Blender (Figure 1.18).

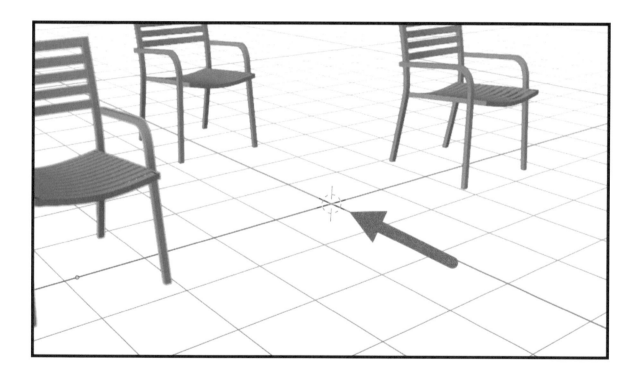

Figure 1.18 - *3D Cursor*

With the 3D Cursor you can:

– Set the location where you create 3D objects

– Move objects to a certain location

– Work as a temporary pivot point for rotation and scaling

Those are a few functions for the 3D Cursor, which you use a lot for modeling and object manipulation. Since that is a core function of Blender, you must learn how to move and align the Cursor around the 3D Viewport.

1.6.1 Moving the 3D Cursor

The 3D Cursor is important for several different types of tasks related to modeling and manipulating objects, and you must know how to move it around. You can easily set the location of your 3D Cursor using the mouse.

Hold down the SHIFT key and right-click anywhere in your 3D Viewport to set a new 3D Cursor location. There is even an option at the 3D Viewport Toolbar that will enable you to left-click without the SHIFT key to set a new location for the 3D Cursor (Figure 1.19).

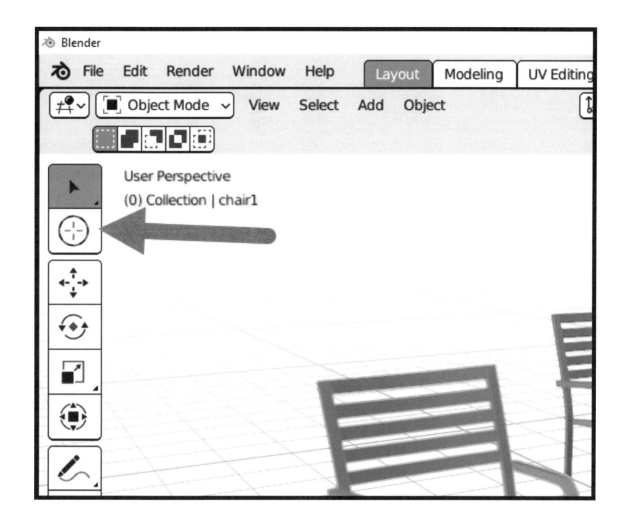

Figure 1.19 - *3D Cursor in the Toolbar*

Even with those options to quickly move your 3D Cursor using the mouse, you will probably want to have more control over the cursor location.

You can have precise control on the 3D Cursor location using the Sidebar of your 3D Viewport. By pressing the N key, you will open the Sidebar, and at the View tab, you will find the 3D Cursor options (Figure 1.20).

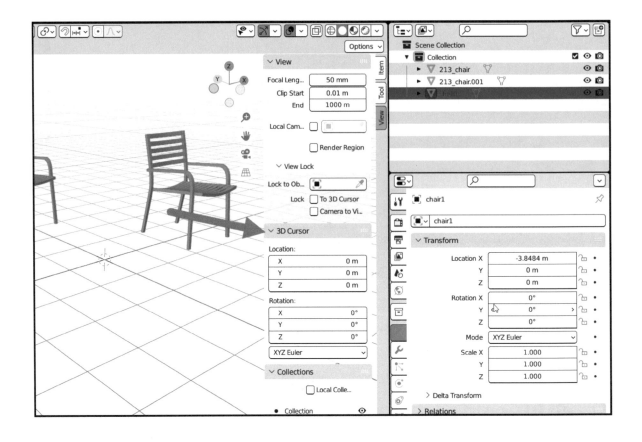

Figure 1.20 - 3D Cursor options

There you can change the values for both location and rotation of your 3D Cursor. An important shortcut to handle the 3D Cursor is the SHIFT+C, which will center the 3D Cursor in your 3D Viewport and align your view to the Cursor.

The shortcut works like a reset for the 3D Cursor, and you should use it whenever you want to get it back to the origin point of your 3D Viewport.

1.6.2 Using the Snap for the 3D Cursor

By using the selection tools and our 3D Cursor, we can move objects in the 3D Viewport with the Snap options of Blender. What is the Snap? That is a collection of tools that will allow you to align and move certain objects using certain rules.

For instance, you can get a selected object to move to the same location as your 3D Cursor. You can also align the Cursor with an object location.

To use your Snap options in Blender, you will use either the **Object → Snap** menu or the SHIFT+S keys. When you press the keys, the Snap options appears (Figure 1.21).

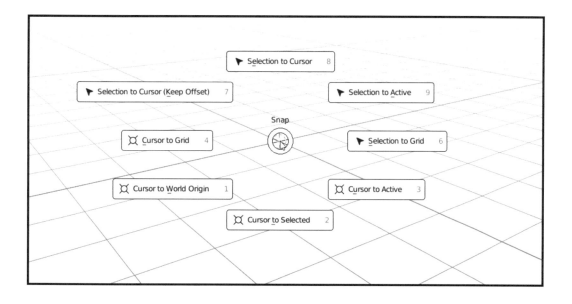

Figure 1.21 - *Snap options*

At the Snap, you will find the following options:

– **Selection to Cursor**: Move the selected object to the 3D Cursor location.

– **Selection to Active**: Move the selected object to the same position as your active object.

– **Selection to Grid**: Align the selected object to the grid lines at the base of your 3D Viewport.

– **Cursor to Active**: Align the 3D Cursor to the Active object.

– **Cursor to Selected**: Move the 3D Cursor to the same location of your selected object.

– **Cursor to World Origin**: Move the 3D Cursor to the zero coordinate for X, Y, and Z.

– **Cursor to Grid**: Align the 3D Cursor to the grid lines at the base of your 3D Viewport.

– **Selection to Cursor (Keep offset)**: Moves the selected object to the 3D Cursor location and keeps the positions relative to each vertex of your 3D model. We will cover more about vertex manipulation in chapter 3.

How to use the Snap to manipulate objects? You can move any selected objects to the 3D Cursor location using the Snap. For instance, we can take the scene shown in Figure 1.22.

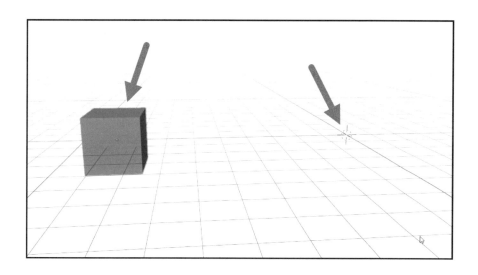

Figure 1.22 - *Using the Snap*

We have an object at the scene that is far away from the 3D Cursor. If you press the SHIFT+S keys and from the Snap options choose **Selection to Cursor**, you will make the object "jump" to the location of your 3D Cursor (Figure 1.23).

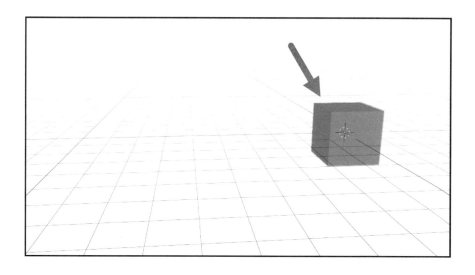

Figure 1.23 - *Object aligned to 3D Cursor*

You can also choose the **Cursor to Selection** to make your 3D Cursor move to the object location (Figure 1.24).

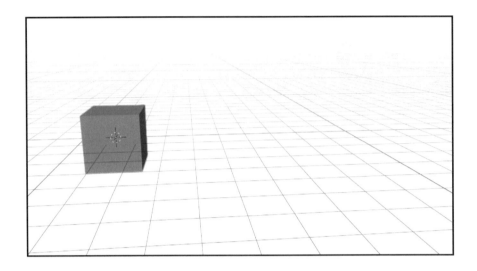

Figure 1.24 - *3D Cursor aligned to the object*

It may look simple now to have a tool dedicated to moving objects in the 3D Viewport. But you will see the importance of the 3D Cursor when we start to work with object creation and modeling in chapters 2 and 3.

Info: The reference point for object locations in Blender have the name of Origin Point. We will learn how to manipulate and control those points in chapter 2.

1.7 Using the status bar

At the very bottom of your user interface, we have a status bar that is useful to give you additional information about a tool or the current scene. For instance, when pressing the B key to start a box selection, it will give you some information or additional options for that tool (Figure 1.25).

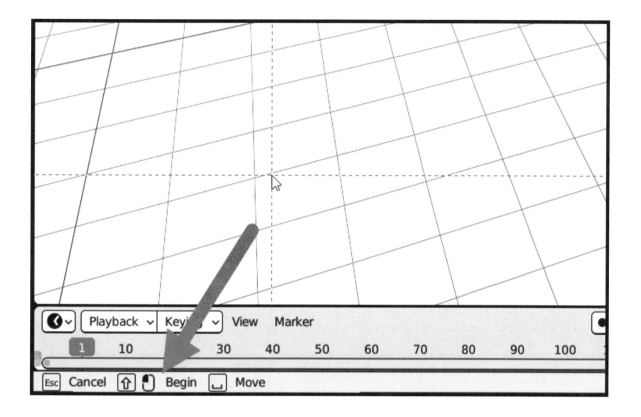

Figure 1.25 - Additional tools and options

Those additional tools and options appear on the left side of the status bar, and it adapts to the tool you are using at the moment. Always keep an eye there to find new shortcuts and options.

On the right side, we have, by default, only the Blender version. You can add more information by right-clicking there to open a small menu (Figure 1.26).

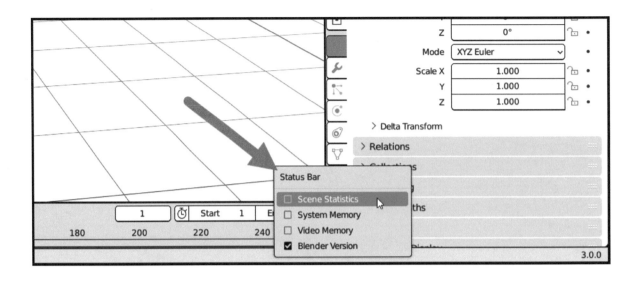

Figure 1.26 - *Status bar information*

For instance, if you enable all options from the menu, you will have some useful information about the Blender file displayed (Figure 1.27).

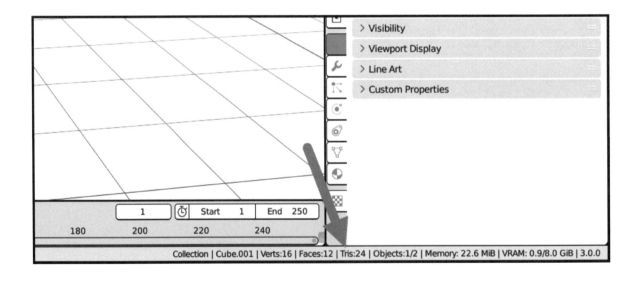

Figure 1.27 - *Scene information*

There you have a list with statistics about your 3D models like:

– Objects

– Faces

– Triangles

– Vertices

Besides that, you have two important information about the scene. One is the current memory used by Blender to edit the project. You can keep an eye on this value in systems that have limited memory available.

Another option that can make a difference later during rendering is the VRAM amount. If you have a dedicated graphics card in your computer, it has a total amount of memory. To render a scene with GPU acceleration, Blender needs to load the scene to that memory.

The scene must fit inside the memory for processing, and the VRAM information helps you keep track of that limit. If it doesn't fit, you must render the scene with CPU only, which is slower in most cases.

You only see the VRAM value in Blender if you have a dedicated graphics card and a driver that gives access to that information.

What is next?

Now that you have a solid understanding of the basic aspects of Blender, it is time practice. Use the default starting scene and try to move around in the 3D Viewport. By triggering keyboard shortcuts or navigation icons, you start memorizing those options.

With practice and a few minutes of work, it will soon become something you do without thinking about it. For instance, if you have to set the 3D Viewport to the top orthographic view, your hand will go to the Numpad 7 and Numpad 5 keys.

Experienced Blender artists usually interact with the keyboard and interface without stopping and thinking about what key they must press for a task. After using Blender for a while, you will also develop a "navigational memory."

In the next chapter, you will start to work with object creation, manipulation, and transformations.

Chapter 2 - Object creation and manipulation

After you start manipulating objects in the 3D Viewport, the next step is to go beyond simple selections and move to basic modeling and transformations. In this chapter, we start using some of the tools Blender has to transform 3D objects.

A transformation in a 3D space could be either a move, rotation, or scale. Those are the three fundamental transformations we can apply to any tridimensional element or object.

By using those transformations, you will be able to reorganize a scene and place objects whenever you want. Besides transformations, you also learn how to add new objects in the 3D Viewport.

At the end of this chapter, you will feel more comfortable with 3D object manipulation and creation.

Here is a list of what you will learn:

– How to create objects in the 3D Viewport

– Duplicate existing objects

– Use transformations like move, rotate, and scale

– Take advantage of the Undo history of Blender

– Start using Edit Mode for object manipulation

– Control object origins with the Snap

– Move objects with precision using the 3D Cursor

– Organize objects into collections

– Rename objects

2.1 Creating objects in Blender

To create objects in Blender, you will have to either use the **Add** menu that appears at the 3D Viewport header or the SHIFT+A keys. The shortcut works for object creation when you have the 3D Viewport as the Active Editor if you don't remember how Active Editors works, go back to chapter 1 and reread section 1.3.

By pressing SHIFT+A or opening the Add menu, you will see a box with all creation options for Blender (Figure 2.1).

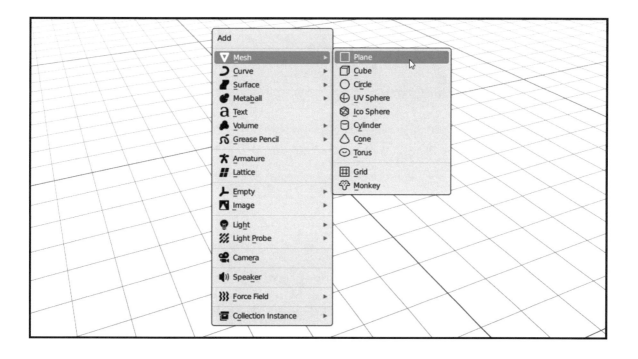

Figure 2.1 - Object creation box

You will find options to add different types of objects in that menu, starting with polygons under the Mesh group and others like cameras, lights, and even Collection instances. Depending on the project in Blender, you might need a particular type of object. To get started with 3D modeling, the most straightforward type to create and manage is a Mesh object (Polygon).

At the Mesh group, you can create geometrical primitives such as:

– Plane

– Cube

– Circle

– UV Sphere (square faces)

– ICO Sphere (triangular facer)

– Cylinder

– Cone

– Torus

We can use those primitives as a starting point for several modeling projects. A Cube can become a chair or a human-head depending on the number of modifications applied to the object.

To create a model at the 3D Viewport, you must pick a location to create the object by placing the 3D Cursor and pressing the SHIFT+A keys or using the Add menu. For instance, we can add a new Cylinder to the scene (Figure 2.2).

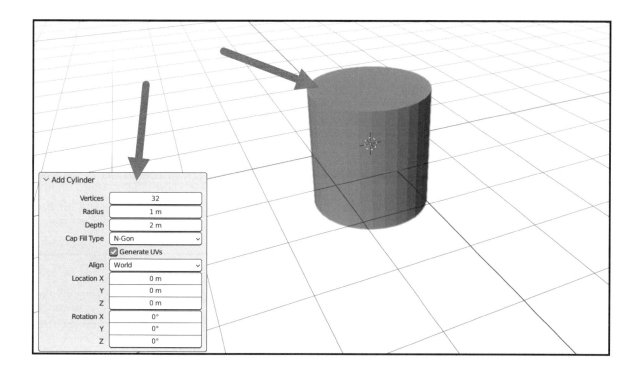

Figure 2.2 - *Cylinder at the scene*

One important aspect of the object creation is that every time you add an object to the 3D Viewport, a small menu appears at the lower-left corner of your 3D Viewport. That menu displays some contextual information regarding the created object.

For instance, when you create a Cylinder, it is possible to edit aspects of the object like:

– **Vertices**: The number of sides for the cylinder.

– **Radius**: Distance from the center to the border.

– **Depth**: The height of your cylinder.

If you plan or need to make changes to the object based on that contextual menu, you must do it right after the object creation. If you select anything else or perform another operation, that menu disappears.

Tip: If you accidentally close the menu by selecting other objects, you can call it back by pressing the F9 key. However, it will only work if you don't perform any other operation. The F9 key calls the "Adjust last operation…" option.

In some cases, you must use the menu to make adjustments to the object. For instance, you can create a square from a Circle. Create a Circle from the Mesh group and set your Vertices option to four (Figure 2.3).

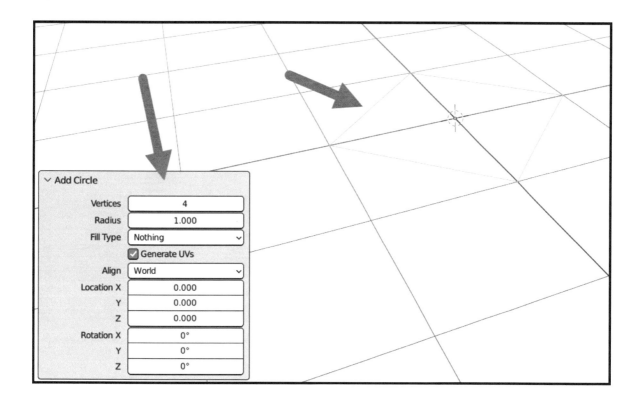

Figure 2.3 - *Square from circle*

That results in a square, which is similar to a Mesh Plane that only has border edges.

For each object created in Blender, it is possible to view and edit some of their properties straight in the 3D Viewport. For that, you must use the Sidebar by pressing the N key (Figure 2.4).

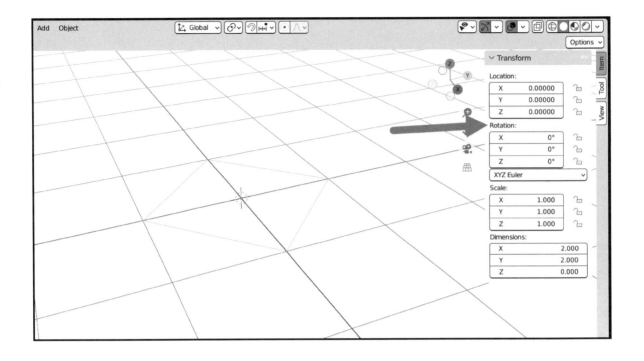

Figure 2.4 - *Sidebar*

Those properties are different from the ones in the small contextual menu. At the Sidebar, you get general objects properties.

By selecting an object, you will be able to change properties like:

– Location

– Rotation

– Scale

Each property has numeric values that can receive updates in each respective field. For instance, you can rotate an object in the Z-axis 45 degrees by entering that value in the Rotation text field identified with the Z letter.

Tip: When you press the N key to expand the 3D Viewport Sidebar, your mouse cursor must be above the 3D Viewport Editor. Other Editors also feature Sidebars with different properties.

You will also find the same options in the Properties Editor, where you have the Object Properties tab (Figure 2.5).

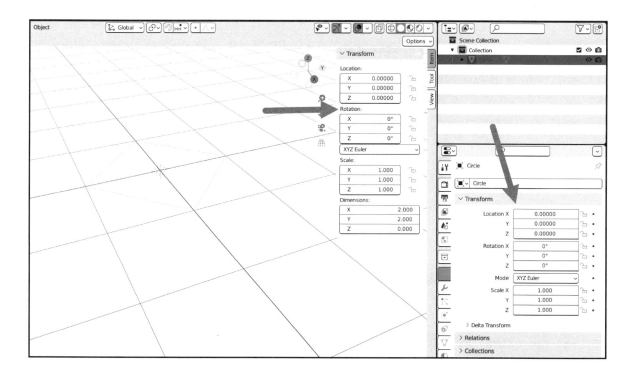

Figure 2.5 - Properties Editor

Both options display information based on the selected objects. The Sidebar has a shorter list of options, whereas, with the Properties Editor, you will get extended options to edit objects spread across multiple tabs.

Tip: *Regardless of the method, you can activate an interesting tool to protect objects from receiving transformations. You can enable the small padlock icon for each transformation to protect them from any unintentional changes.*

2.2 Object transformations

After you start creating objects in Blender, you will probably want to make some transformations in the 3D Viewport. In any software that supports the handling of 3D Data, you will most likely find three main types of transformations:

- Move

- Rotate

- Scale

Those transformations will help you in tasks like modeling and also scene organization. There are multiple options to apply 3D transformations in Blender. One of them is the gizmo that appears after choosing a transformation from the Toolbar (Figure 2.6).

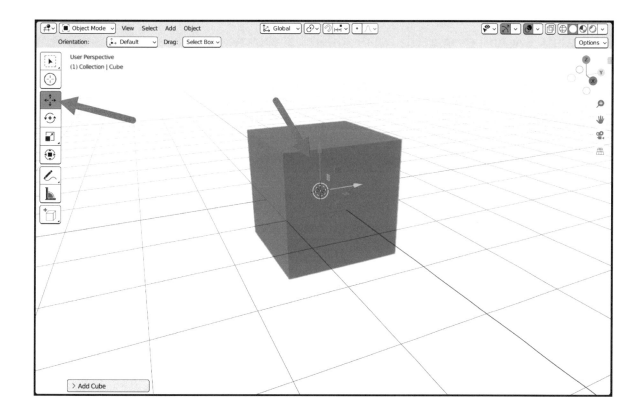

Figure 2.6 - *Transform gizmo*

The gizmo icon changes based on the transformation type you choose from the Toolbar. Each gizmo allows interaction with a selected object in a certain way:

– **Move**: Click and drag the mouse on the arrow corresponding to the axis in which you want to move the object.

– **Rotate**: Click and drag the mouse in the arc representing the axis you want to use for a rotation.

– **Scale**: Click and drag in the small squares at the end of each line representing an axis.

A quick way to change the gizmo type is with the SHIFT+SPACEBAR keys. By pressing those keys in the 3D Viewport, you will open a small menu with shortcuts for all three transformations. There is also an option with the name of Transform, which will create a "super" gizmo with all three operations appearing simultaneously.

Tip: You can toggle the 3D Viewport Toolbar using the T key. By default, you will only see vertical icons as the Toolbar, but you can expand it by placing the mouse cursor at the right border of your icons. Once it turns to a double-sided arrow, you can click and drag to expand.

Even with the gizmo offering a visual tool to apply transformations, you will find that most artists using Blender prefer to use keyboard shortcuts to perform transformations. You can quickly implement a transformation using the following shortcuts:

– **G key**: Move an object

– **R key**: Rotate an object

– **S key**: Scale an object

Once you trigger a transformation using those keys, click somewhere in the 3D Viewport to finish an operation. For instance, select one or multiple objects and press the G key. By moving your mouse cursor, all selected objects will follow the same movement. With a left-click, you confirm the new location for your selected objects.

At any moment, you can also cancel the transformation by pressing the ESC key.

Tip: Those keys work in all editors for transformations. For instance, you can move animation data in the Timeline using the G key.

As you will quickly realize, after trying to apply a transformation with a key, it will occur in all axis at the same time. The objects transform freely in your 3D Viewport, unlike the gizmo, where you can choose the axis by color to apply it.

There is a way to constraint any transformation to an axis by pressing the corresponding axis key you wish to use. For instance, you can move an object in the X-axis by pressing the X key after you hit the G key.

Here are some examples of keys that apply transformations with an axis constraint:

– **G key followed by the Y key**: Move in the Y-axis

– **R key followed by the Z key**: Rotate in the Z-axis

– **S key followed by the X key**: Scale in the X-axis

Notice that you should press the keys in sequence and not at the same time. You can use any combination of those keys to apply a transformation.

Tip: You can always cancel the current transformation by pressing the ESC key.

All transformation options are also available at the **Object → Transformations** menu. There you will find a list with additional tools regarding object transformation in Blender.

2.2.1 Duplicating objects

In Blender, you will find that some operations will automatically trigger a transformation. For instance, if you duplicate an object in your 3D Viewport, it will also move the copied object to a new location. You can use the same shortcuts and options from transformations, like constraint them to a single axis.

First, how to duplicate an object? To create a duplicate of any object, you can use the SHIFT+D keys with an object selected or use the **Object → Duplicate Objects** menu. For instance, you can choose one or multiple objects and press the SHIFT+D keys. By moving the mouse cursor, you will start to see the duplicates. Click anywhere in your 3D Viewport to place your newly created objects.

If you want to create a more ordinated set of copies, you can press a key corresponding to an axis in your keyboard, right after pressing SHIFT+D. You can create multiple copies of objects in the X-axis using the X key right after pressing SHIFT+D (Figure 2.7).

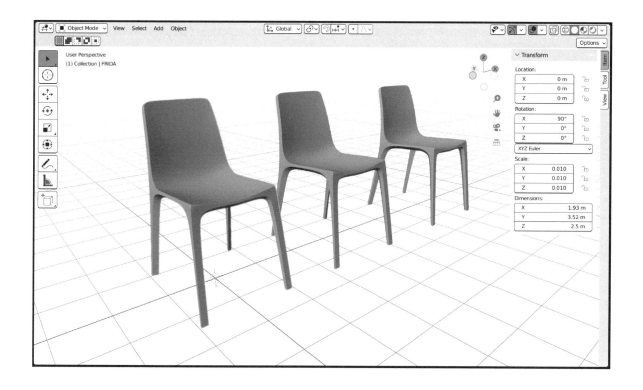

Figure 2.7 - *Copies in the X-axis*

Using the SHIFT+D keys gives you a lot of freedom to create all kinds of copies based on the type of selection you have in Blender. For instance, you can start making multiple copies from a selection of various objects at the same time.

There is also another option for duplicating objects called Linked Duplicate. By making a linked copy, you make an instance of your selected object. Any changes applied to one object propagates to all copies. Use the ALT+D to create a linked copy.

To unlink any duplicates created with the ALT+D, use the **Object** → **Relations** → **Make Single User** → **Object & Data** menu. Select the copied object and use that menu option.

Info: For some operations, you might want to create a copy of an object that is in the same location as your original selection. By pressing the ESC key after SHIFT+D, you create the duplicate but cancel the move transformation. That results in your objects staying at the same locations.

2.2.2 Numeric transformations

One option that you can use in Blender to enhance your transformations is to use numeric values to set distances, rotations, and scale factors. Whenever you trigger a transformation in Blender, you can type in your keyboard to assign precise values for that particular transformation.

For instance, you can press the R key to rotate and limit it to the Z-axis (Z key), and once you move the mouse, values for that rotation will appear at the status bar of the 3D Viewport (Figure 2.8).

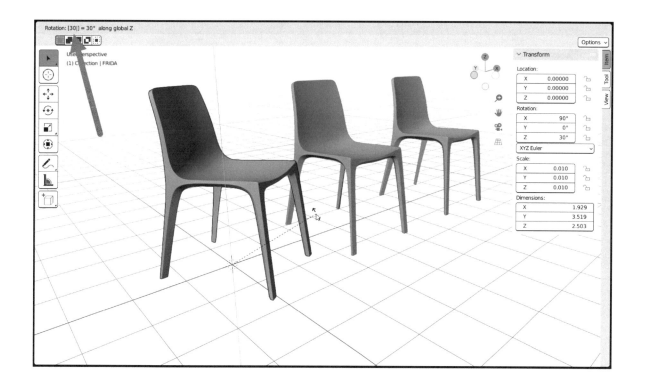

Figure 2.8 - *Rotation values*

Notice that this is a different status bar, which appears on the top left of your 3D Viewport. Back in chapter 1, we saw the status bar dedicated to displaying information about the project and tools on the bottom of your interface.

If you type a value like 45 and press RETURN before clicking anywhere, you set the rotation to a precise value of 45 degrees (Figure 2.9).

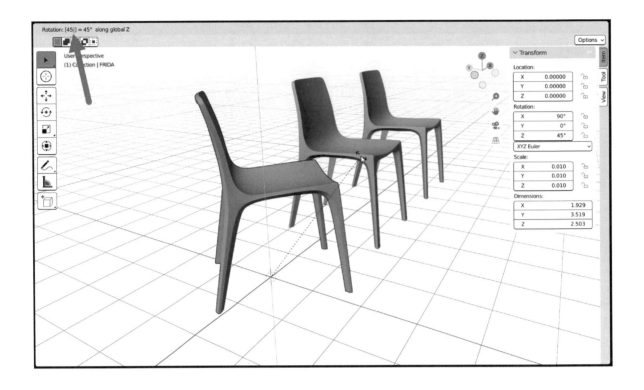

Figure 2.9 - Rotation with fixed value

You can verify the rotation amount in the Sidebar. Look to the Rotation field with the object selected, and in your Z-axis, it should display 45. There you can also make changes to that transformation by setting a different value in the Sidebar.

The same applies to a move transformation, where you can:

1. Select an object

2. Press the G key to move

3. Press the X key to constrain it to the X-axis

4. Type 5

5. Press RETURN to finish the transformation

That will move your object five units on the X-axis. You can also use negative values by typing -5 to go in the opposite direction.

With the scale, you have to use a factor to control object sizes. For instance, a factor of 1 means 100% of the object size. If you want to increase the size by 50%, use a factor of 1.5 for the scale. To reduce the size by 30%, use 0.7 as a factor.

The sequence to increase the size in 50% would be:

1. Select an object

2. Press the S key to start a scaling transformation

3. Type 1.5

4. Press RETURN to finish the transformation

Notice how we did not constrain the scale to any axis in the sequence, but you could also press a key corresponding to an axis after the S key.

Tip: *You can use either the Sidebar of your 3D Viewport or the Object Properties tab at the Properties Editor to change those values. But, editing with keyboard shortcuts will be much faster.*

2.3 Undoing and Redoing in Blender

How to undo a transformation in Blender? Like most softwares, we also have an Undo option in Blender, which you can use with the CTRL+Z keys. There is an option to trigger the Undo with the **Edit → Undo** menu.

To go back and redo an action, you can use the Redo option, which works using the SHIFT+CTRL+Z keys. Another useful tool in Blender is the Repeat Last option, which you can trigger using the SHIFT+R keys.

The Repeat Last can become useful in some modeling tasks. For instance, if you move an object six units in the X-axis and press SHIFT+R, you will get the same operation repeated.

Instead of applying a single move transformation, you can press SHIFT+R multiple times to repeat the operation.

An essential option regarding undo and redos involve the editing history that Blender keeps for each file you are working at. It is possible to access that history at any moment using the **Edit → Undo History** menu. By choosing that option, you see a list with all recent actions from that file (Figure 2.10).

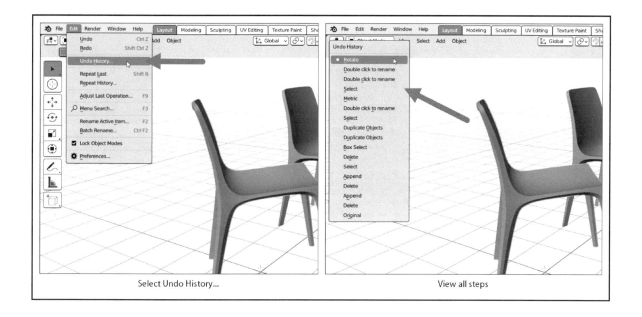

Select Undo History...   View all steps

Figure 2.10 - *Undo history*

Suppose you click at any of those actions, Blender jump back to that state of your project. That is an easy and fast way to undo multiple steps at once.

In addition to that option, you can also control the number of steps Blender keeps in the Undo History. Open the **Edit → Preferences** menu and go to the System tab (Figure 2.11).

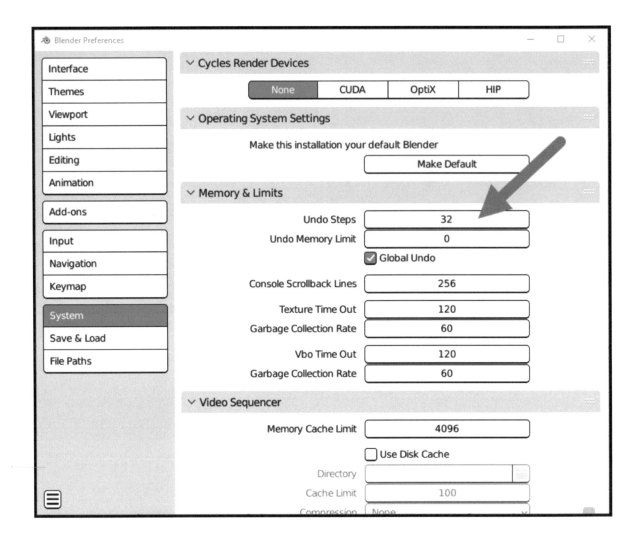

Figure 2.11 - *System options*

There you will find an option called Undo Steps, which starts with 32 as the default value. Increasing that number will make Blender keep more actions and use more memory from your computer. Unless you have a good reason to increase that value, it is wise to leave it with the default number.

Tip: *Even with the option to work with an undo history. You should keep a healthy habit of saving your project as much as possible. That will prevent you from losing data.*

2.4 Work modes

Most entities in Blender, like 3D objects, allows the use of different work modes. Until this moment, you probably used only Object Mode for general object manipulation. Besides Object Mode, we also have other modes like Edit Mode, Sculpt Mode, and Texture Paint.

You can easily see all work modes available for a particular entity using the work mode selector in the 3D Viewport header (Figure 2.12). The selector displays all work modes available for any selected object.

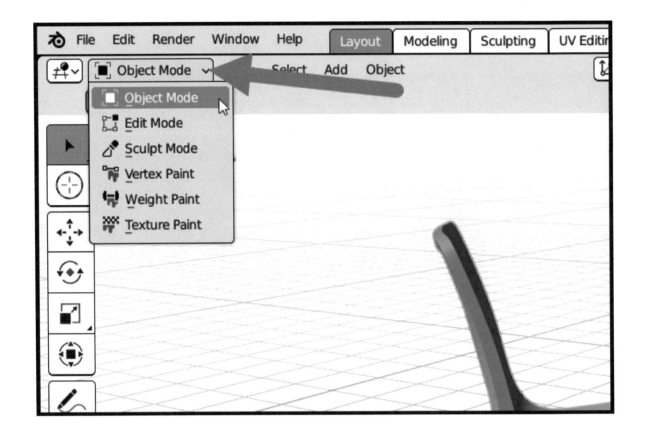

Figure 2.12 - Work mode selector

For instance, a Mesh object shows several types of work modes, and others like a camera will only have Object Mode.

With work modes, we have access to unique tools and options regarding objects manipulation. For Mesh objects, you have Edit Mode, which is the mode where we can perform a significant amount of 3D Modeling in Blender.

Once you select any Mesh object and change the work mode to Edit, you start to see the structure of that selected object. The Toolbar on the left display options related to that mode, and you will be able to view and manipulate:

– Vertices

– Edges

– Faces

You can easily change the type of element you wish to edit for that polygon using the buttons on the right of your work mode selector (Figure 2.13).

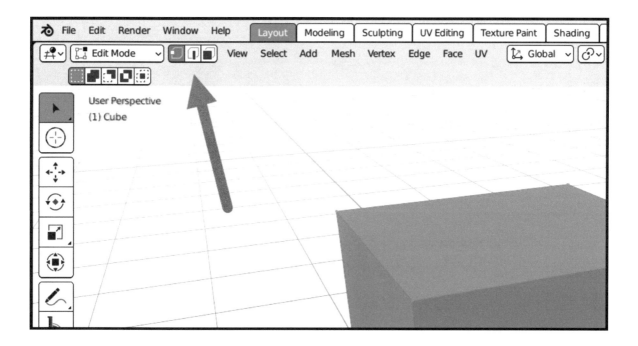

Figure 2.13 - *Mesh element selector*

For instance, you can set the tool to select faces and easily click at any face of a polygon to add it to the selection. You can even mix elements by turning two or three at the same time. To enable multiple elements, hold the SHIFT key while clicking at each button (Figure 2.14).

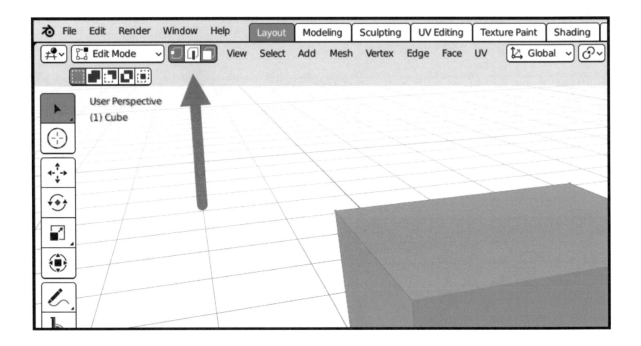

Figure 2.14 - Mixing elements

After selecting an element for a Mesh object, you can apply any transformation to change the structure of that object. It could be a scale or move transformation, which is the starting point for many 3D modeling projects (Figure 2.15).

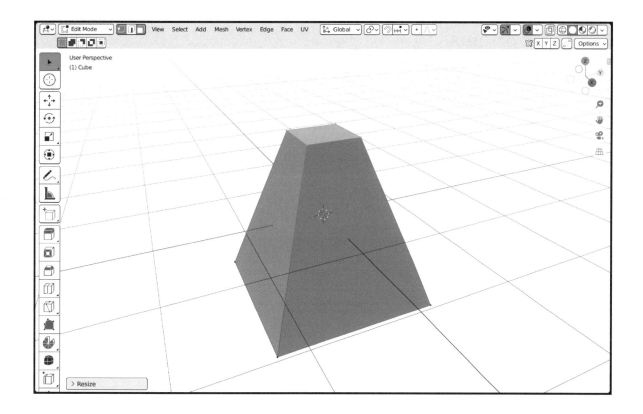

Figure 2.15 - *Object transformation*

The two most used work modes in Blender are the Object and Edit. For that reason, you will find a dedicated shortcut that allows us to quickly swap between those two modes. You can press the TAB key with one or more objects selected, and it will either go to Object or Edit Modes.

If you are in Object Mode, the shortcut swap to Edit Mode, and if you are in Edit Mode, the TAB key will make you go back to Object Mode.

Info: You can use the same shortcuts to select multiple elements. For instance, you can hold the SHIFT key to add multiple elements (vertices, edges, or faces) to the selection.

2.5 Object origins

Before working with 3D modeling in Blender, it is important to understand and learn how to manipulate some key properties of objects in the 3D Viewport. One of those aspects is the object origin point, which might help you place and edit objects with improved precision.

Where are object origins? You will find that most 3D objects in Blender display a small dot with an orange color (Figure 2.16).

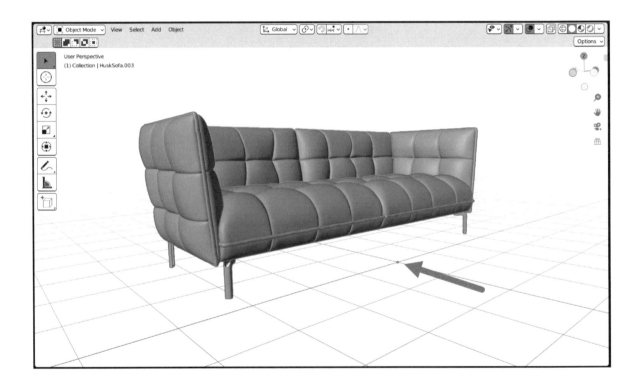

Figure 2.16 - Object origin

Every time you set the coordinates of an object using either the Sidebar or the Properties Editor, you are using the origin point location as the reference. If you set the coordinates to zero for all axis, it will be the origin point that will stay at those coordinates.

For instance, when you create a Cube object with the 3D Cursor at the origin of your scene, which has a zero value for all 3D axis, you will have the Cube placed at the exact center of your scene (Figure 2.17).

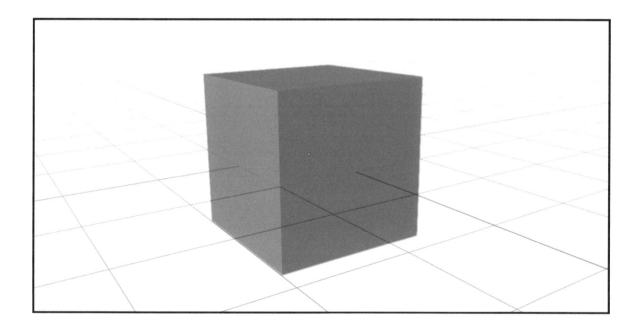

Figure 2.17 - Cube at exact center

Since the origin point for the Cube is in the middle of the object, you have an object with the bottom half below the "ground plane" if you consider that your Z-axis zero level is the ground or floor for your scene (Figure 2.18).

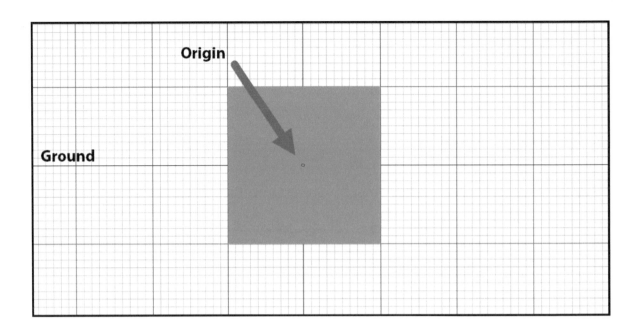

Figure 2.18 - *Object at ground level*

That won't help in tasks where you have to align and place an object at the "ground floor" for modeling. We can easily change and edit the origin point location using a combination of our 3D Cursor and the Snap options.

The Snap options offer a collection of shortcuts that align and set the 3D Cursor with a selected object. You can even use the 3D Cursor as a reference to set a new location for an origin point. That gives us a powerful option to place the origin point in key locations.

For instance, we can place the origin point at the base of the cube using a simple procedure:

1. Select the cube and go to Edit Mode

2. Change the selection mode to face

3. Select the bottom Face of your Cube

4. Press SHIFT+S and choose *Cursor to Selected*

With that procedure, you will get the 3D Cursor aligned to the bottom face of your Cube (Figure 2.19).

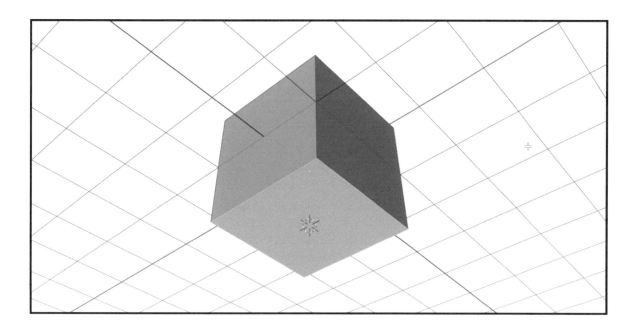

Figure 2.19 *- 3D Cursor aligned to the Cube*

After you align the 3D Cursor, you can go back to Object Mode and use the **Object → Set Origin** menu. There you have an option called **Origin to 3D Cursor**. If you choose that option, you can change the location of your origin point to be the same location as your 3D Cursor (Figure 2.20).

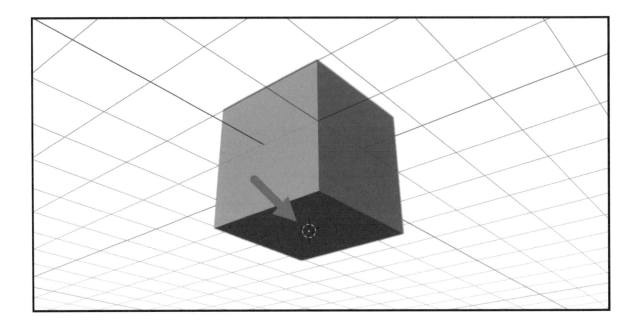

Figure 2.20 - Origin point location

If you try to set a Z coordinate value of the Cube to zero, it will become aligned to the "ground level" of your scene.

You can also use this same technique to place objects in the scene. For instance, we easily place a Cube with an origin point at their bottom face on top of another Cube or any other objects. Make sure the 3D Cursor is at the same location in which you want to align the object to use this procedure.

In that case, we have the Cube with the origin point at the bottom and another larger Cube with the 3D Cursor aligned to the top face (Figure 2.21).

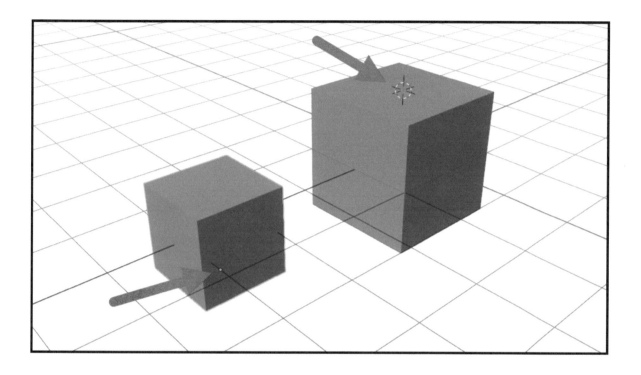

Figure 2.21 - Cubes for alignment

Select the Cube you wish to move and press SHIFT+S and pick *Selection to Cursor*. It makes the selected Cube jump to the 3D Cursor location (Figure 2.22).

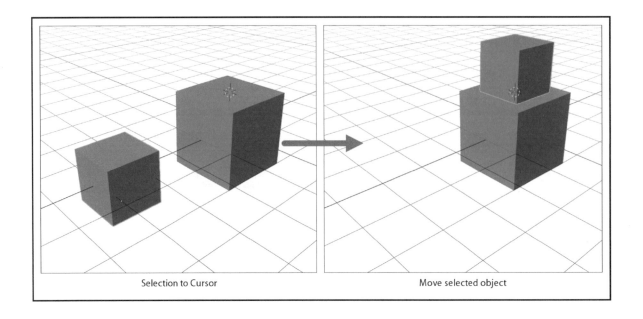

Selection to Cursor   Move selected object

Figure 2.22 - *Cubes after the Snap*

Since our Cube's origin point is at the bottom, it will sit perfectly on top of the other object. You can use the same workflow to move and align other 3D models.

Tip: *Always use the Snap to move and align objects with precision. The Snap also works in Edit Mode for elements like edges and faces.*

2.5.1 Pivot points and transformations

The origin point can assume additional functions in object manipulation, like defining a pivot point for transformations like rotation and scaling. For instance, if you select an object that has the origin point in their center, you will get a rotation happening from that pivot, and all scaling operations will either expand or shrink based on that point (Figure 2.23).

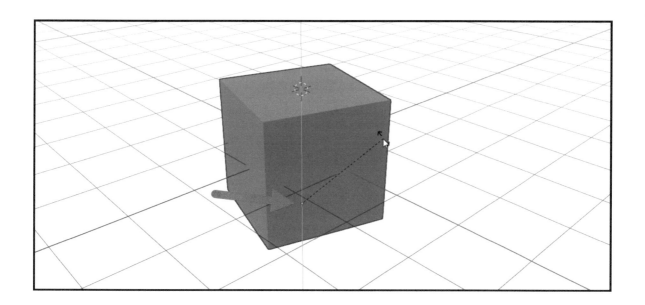

Figure 2.23 - *Pivot example*

That will always happen if you use the default settings for pivot points. By default, Blender uses the Median Point of a selection as the pivot. At the 3D Viewport header, you will find the options for pivot points in Blender (Figure 2.24).

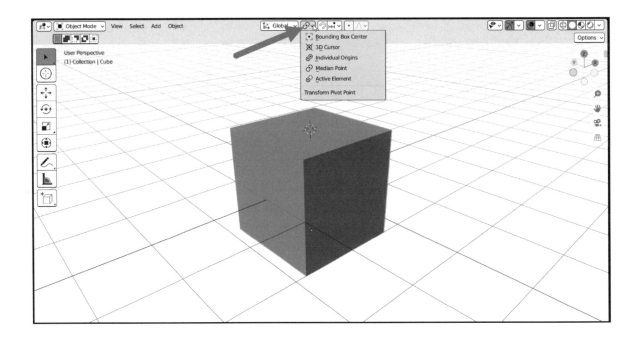

Figure 2.24 - *Pivot options*

There you can set different ways to handle pivot points:

- **Bounding Box Center**: You will use a cube projection shape based on all objects you have in a selection. The center of that projection will be the pivot point.

- **3D Cursor**: The 3D Cursor location will be your pivot point when you use this option.

- **Individual Origins**: When you have multiple objects selected, you will be able to use each origin point as a pivot. The option is great to apply a rotation or scale to various objects as if they were single selections.

– **Median Point**: The default option uses an object origin point for single selections or the median point between multiple selected objects.

– **Active Element**: If you have various objects selected, you can use the active object's origin as a pivot. The active object is always the last one selected.

The management of pivot points in Blender is an option that can save you a lot of time if used correctly. For instance, if you look at the model shown in Figure 2.25, you will see a chair. The origin point for that model is close to the top, not ideal for that type of object.

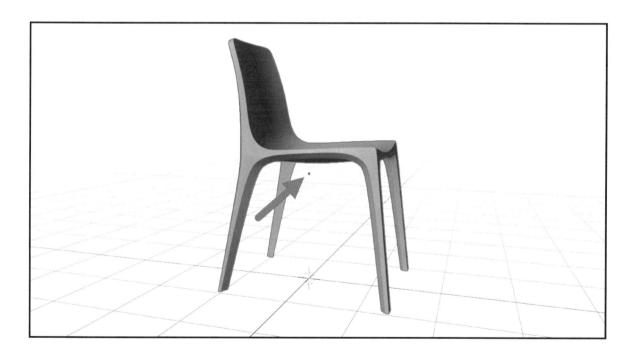

Figure 2.25 - Chair model

Since the model usually aligns with the floor from their bottom, you should place the origin point. Keeping the origin point in any other location might add extra editing steps every time you have to either scale or rotate the object.

Remember that in a scale transformation, you get the object contracting or expanding using the origin as a reference (Figure 2.26).

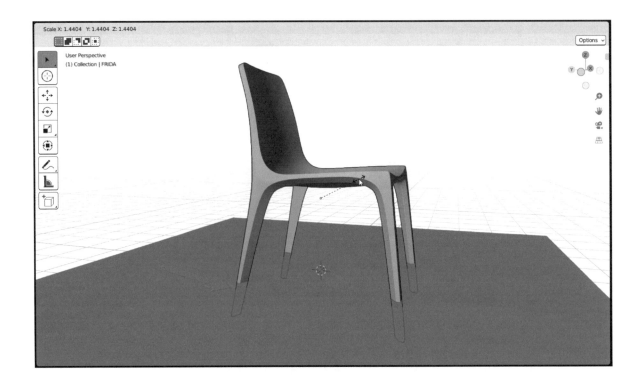

Figure 2.26 - Scale example

After applying a scale using a pivot located anywhere but the bottom, you will have to move the object and align your model with the floor again since the scale changes the size for each chair leg. To avoid that extra editing step, place the origin point at the bottom.

It will make the model scale up and down and keep the legs always above the floor (Figure 2.27).

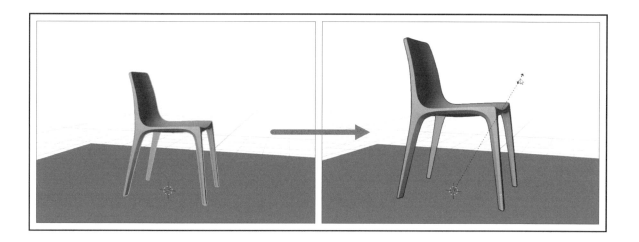

Figure 2.27 - Scale using the bottom as pivot

You can either move the origin point to that location or align the 3D Cursor to the bottom vertices and change pivot settings to use that location. However, you should try to set the origin point of objects in a location where they might get an advantage in modeling tasks.

For an object that should stay above a surface, the best location will always be the contact point between the model and a surface (Figure 2.28).

Figure 2.28 - *Chair model*

The chair model should have the origin point at the bottom because it is the most probable place you will use to align it with the floor.

Tip: The origin point is the insertion location for objects you bring from external files using the Append or Link options. If you have plans to reuse a model, it is even more important to set the best possible origin point.

2.6 Object collections

After you start creating objects, the 3D Viewport will probably become crowded with lots of 3D Models. In Blender, we can work with a tool called Collections that lets you create something similar to groups. By using Collections, you have much better control over complex scenes.

The Collections appears in the Outliner Editor in the top right of your default user interface (Figure 2.29).

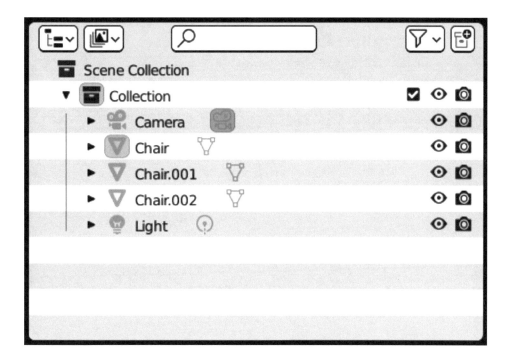

Figure 2.29 - Outliner Editor

At the Outliner, you have the Scene Collection, which is the base for all Blender files. Even if you don't want to use any new Collections, it will appear as the base for your scene.

You also have a "Collection" that has your default Cube, Camera, and Lamp. All objects you add to the scene will go to the Active Collection. You will see a small greyed circle next to the Collection name showing if it is active (Figure 2.30).

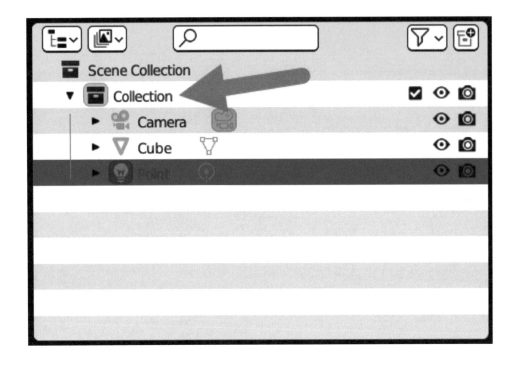

Figure 2.30 - *Active Collection*

To make a Collection active, you can simply click on their name.

Info: You will also see the active Collection name at the top left corner if your 3D Viewport.

You can create new Collections using several different options. In the Outliner Editor, right-click at a space and choose "New" to create a Collection (Figure 2.31).

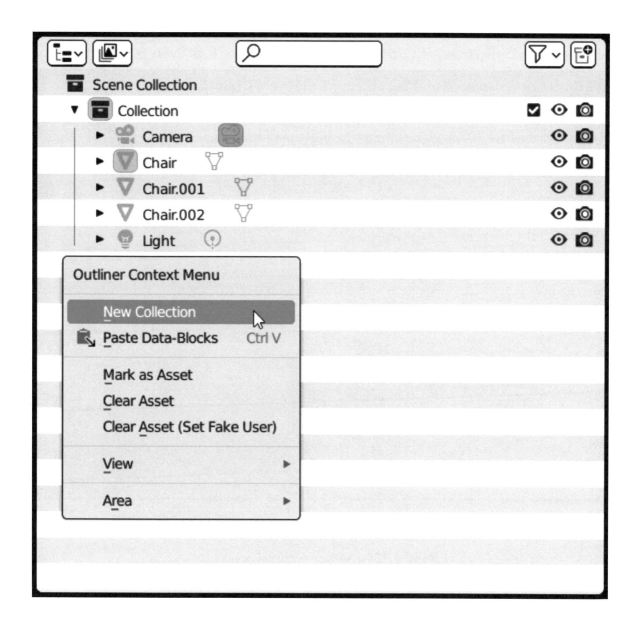

Figure 2.31 - New Collection

With a double-click on any Collection name, you can rename them to something that will help you manage the scene. Still, in the Outliner Editor, you can move objects between Collections with a simple drag and drop. It is even possible to drag and drop full Collections and nest them inside other Collections.

Another way to move and manage Collections is with a shortcut in the 3D Viewport. If you select one or multiple objects and press the M key. It opens a small menu that lets you move the objects to an existing Collection or create a new one (Figure 2.32).

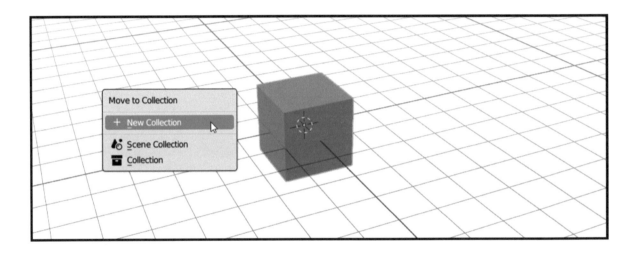

Figure 2.32 - Move to Collection menu

The use of Collections is optional and won't impact your creative results. But, using Collections might give you several benefits:

  – You can put all objects from the same type in a single Collection. For instance, all furniture objects from a scene in a Collection called furniture. That way, you can easily select all objects from a Collection using SHIFT+G.

– At the Collections controls, you can hide objects from a Collection from the 3D Viewport by clicking on the small eye icon. You can hide individual objects or the entire Collection.

– If you click on the eye icon while holding the CTRL key, you hide all other Collections but the one you are clicking. Click again to unhide.

– A Collection appears in the list of objects you can use to append from external files. Using the Append or Link options from the File menu will allow you to get all the contents of one or multiple Collections.

– There is an option to create instances of Collections using the SHIFT+A keys. Locate the Collection Instance option to add an instance of existing Collections.

As you can see from the list, you have multiple benefits by using Collections in your projects. For that reason, it is important to not only use them but assign meaningful names to each of the Collections. That helps to identify what types of objects they hold.

Tip: *You can also use Collections from the Add menu. If you look at the bottom of the menu, you can create new instances from existing collections pressing the SHIFT+A key.*

2.6.1 Renaming objects

As you start to create objects in Blender, you will notice that their names appear as a combination of object type and a numeric sequence. The default Cube displays the name of "Cube," after adding another object of the same kind, it receives the name of "Cube.001".

Unless you rename those objects, after a few hours of work, you might have a scene filled with Cubes starting with "001" and going all the way to "100". That is terrible for scene organization, and you will easily lose control over the project.

To avoid losing control, keep in mind that each object in Blender must have a unique name.

To help manage object names, you have multiple ways to quickly identify the name of any selected object. When you select an object, look at the top left corner. There you find the active Collection and the name of your selected object (Figure 2.33).

Figure 2.33 - Object name selected

It is a good practice to assign unique names to each object to keep the scene organized. Assigning names helps avoid having dozens, hundreds, or thousands of objects with default names followed by a number.

To rename an object, you can:

– **Select the object and press F2**: That calls a small menu that will let you pick a new name.

– **Double-click at the object name in the Outliner Editor**: You can rename the object straight from the Collections list.

– **Use the Properties Editor**: Select the object and go to the Object tab. At the top, you will be able to set a new name.

At the Properties Editor, you will have the object name at the top of that tab (Figure 2.34).

Figure 2.34 - Properties Editor

You should always assign names to your models to help you manage large scenes or bring objects from external files.

Tip: If you have objects with multiple parts, you can use the numeric suffix and place them all into a collection. Later you will be able to select or instance that Collection.

What is next?

After learning about 3D transformations, adding new objects, and work modes, it is time to start creating with Blender. With this new knowledge, you can put your creative mind to work. Add some Mesh primitives and try to deform them in Edit Mode to create unique shapes.

Our next step is to add new objects to a scene and, with Edit Mode, apply transformations and special tools to start making 3D models. One of the easiest ways to start a 3D modeling project is with a primitive like a Cube. We can edit, cut, and change the Cube until it assumes another shape.

That is our goal in the next chapter.

Before we get there, you can go back in chapter 2 and practice with the 3D Cursor and organize the scene in Collections. Move 3D primitives around and try to move them with the Snap and 3D Cursor.

It will be helpful in the following chapters.

Chapter 3 - Tools for 3D modeling

The use of modeling tools in Blender can transform the way you manage and handle 3D objects. We can quickly point the extrude as one of the most important and flexible tools among the options available. With the extrude, we can grab a Mesh object and transform it in many ways.

In this chapter, you will learn how to use the extrude tool to create new shapes based on existing Mesh objects like a Cube or a Cylinder. You also learn how to cut, merge, and connect elements like vertices. Our focus is to give you options to edit and step into 3D modeling.

Those tools will give you a great foundation to 3D modeling, which applies to most projects requiring some degree of 3D creation based on polygons.

Here is a list of what you will learn:

– Use a semi-transparent mode to better select 3D models

– Apply extrudes to 3D objects for modeling

– Work with precision extrudes to create new shapes

– Add cuts to models based on loops of edges

– Connect and create new geometry based on vertices, edges, and faces

– Separate and join models

– Merge elements like vertices to fix 3D models

– Use the mirror mode to invert 3D models

3.1 X-Ray and shading modes for modeling

As you start handling 3D objects in Blender for modeling tasks, it will become important to use a tool called X-Ray to make your selections easier in those contexts. Why is X-Ray mode important for modeling? The mode helps you edit certain types of objects occluded by existing geometry.

For instance, if you get a simple Cube in your 3D Viewport and try to select the bottom vertices using the B Key, you will notice that only the visible vertices become selected. By using X-Ray mode, you can easily select all vertices—even those behind existing faces.

To enable X-Ray Mode, use the button located at the 3D Viewport header, on the left of the shading modes (Figure 3.1).

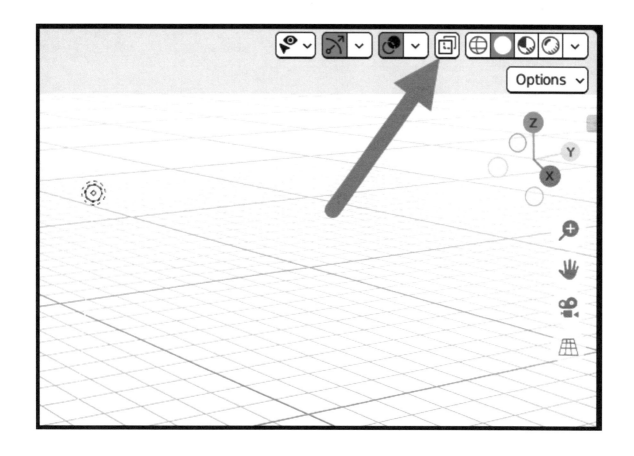

Figure 3.1 - X-Ray Mode

Once you enable X-Ray Mode, you start to see all faces in 3D models as semi-transparent surfaces. As they become transparent, you will select those elements using tools like the B Key (Figure 3.2).

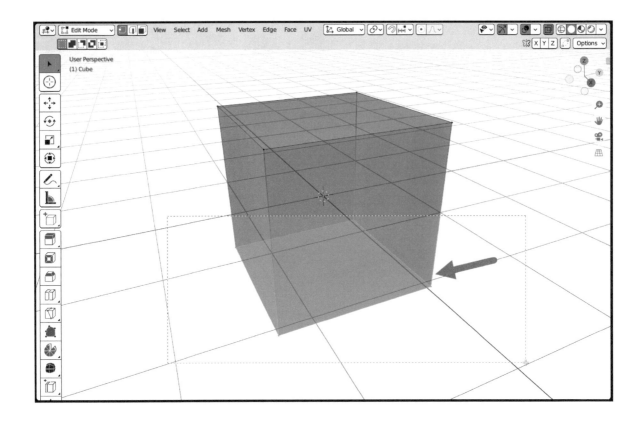

Figure 3.2 - *Using a box selection*

Enabling X-Ray mode gives you the freedom to remain in a shading mode like Solid and still select and interact with elements of your model that are behind faces.

3.1.1 Shading modes

If you don't want to use X-Ray to visualize elements occluded by your 3D model's surfaces, you can also swap between shading modes to help with a selection. Even being a subject related to rendering, you can use those modes to make your modeling tasks easier.

Shading modes are available on the right side of your 3D Viewport header (Figure 3.3). You can also use the Z key to change those modes quickly.

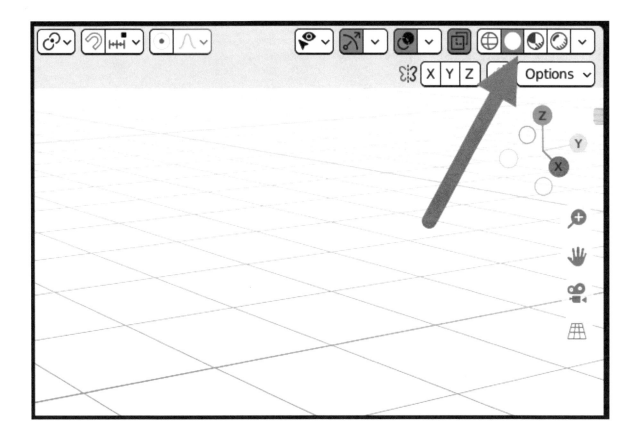

Figure 3.3 - Shading modes

There you can choose from four main shading modes:

– **Wireframe**: A simple mode where you will see your models' polygon structure using only the lines connecting the vertices.

– **Solid**: The default mode for shading where you view models with a solid color for all faces.

– **Material Preview**: Here, we have a mode that shows a simplified version of your lights and displays materials for surfaces.

– **Rendered**: The most advanced mode where you will view shadows, textures, and lights.

It is possible to work in a Rendered mode for your projects. Still, you might experience some performance issues depending on your scene's complexity and the available hardware (Figure 3.4).

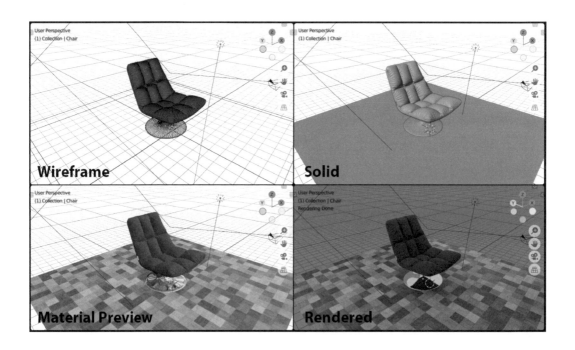

Figure 3.4 - *Shading modes*

For modeling projects, the best approach is to stay between Wireframe and Solid. They offer the best combination of performance and visualization options for your projects. Even in Wireframe mode, you still might have occluded elements based on the location and viewing angle.

Whenever you have parts of a 3D model occluded by existing geometry, enable X-Ray mode to select those parts regardless of your viewing angle.

3.2 Extrude for polygon modeling

Having a geometrical primitive like a Cube or Cylinder in a scene could be great for learning purposes, but you will probably want to modify their shapes to build different objects. Regarding object transformation and modeling, you will find that one option in Blender is among the most used tools for polygon modeling.

The extrude is a tool that allows us to select and expand the shape of a Mesh object. You can select either a vertex, edge, or face to start an extrude. With the extrude, you get a copy of the selected elements connected to the original selection. That is a simple way to describe how it works.

It may sound confusing at first, but after using the extrude for a few times, you will see how it can transform any 3D modeling pipeline. For instance, if we select a face from a Cube and apply an extrude, you will see the results shown in Figure 3.5.

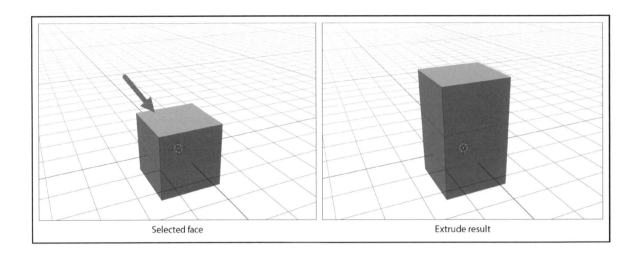

Figure 3.5 - Extrude applied to face

You can also apply an extrude to either a vertex or edge. For a vertex, you will get an edge as a result, and in case you select an edge, it creates a plane (Figure 3.6).

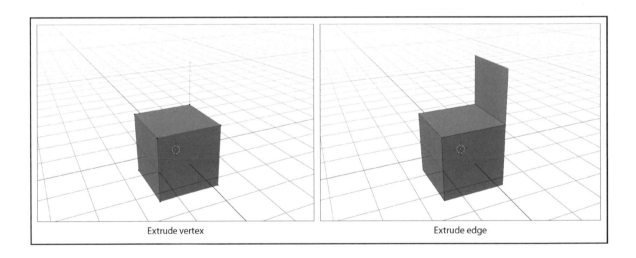

Figure 3.6 - Extrude in vertices and edges

How to use the extrude? The easiest way to trigger an extrude is with the E key in Edit Mode. The shortcut calls the Extrude Region option. After selecting the target elements, you want to extrude, press the E key to start.

If you perform the extrude entirely with the mouse, you must left-click somewhere to end the transformation. That gives you only visual feedback on the length of your resulting shape.

Like the move transformation learned in chapter 2, you can also assign numeric values to each extrude. For instance, if you want to create an extrude of a face with two units in size:

1. Select the face

2. Press the E key

3. Type 2

4. Press RETURN to confirm

All extrudes from faces occur in a perpendicular direction from the selected face (Figure 3.7).

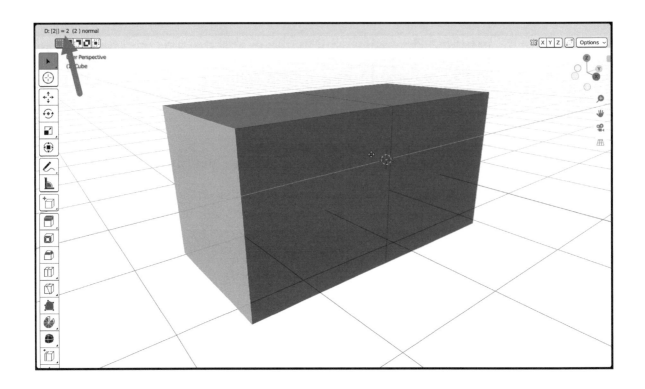

Figure 3.7 - *Extrude with a size of two*

In case you want to extrude from an edge or vertex, you might want to constrain the transformation to an axis.

3.2.1 Extrude modes

Besides the E key, you can also trigger the extrude using the options from the Toolbar. There you will find four buttons with different types of extrudes (Figure 3.8).

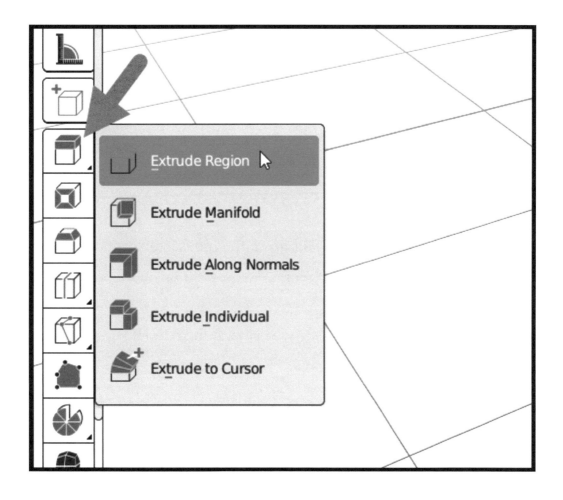

Figure 3.8 - *Extrude in the Toolbar*

Here are all the extrude types:

– **Extrude Region**: Select one or multiple elements to extrude them as a single block. That is the default extrude option you can trigger with the E key.

– **Extrude Manifold**: A powerful new extrude mode introduced with Blender 2.9 that can automatically divide and erase faces based on their location. It is a great tool to extrude to the interior of your existing model.

– **Extrude Along Normals**: The extrude will use the element normals to get a direction. Usually, the normals go towards the perpendicular direction from the selected element.

– **Extrude Individual**: You can create an extrude from multiple elements like you were selecting each one individually. The extrudes will go in a unique direction for each selected element.

– **Extrude to Cursor**: The extrude will go to the mouse cursor location. It will create irregular shapes depending on the cursor position on the screen

Another way to call those different extrudes is with the ALT+E key that brings the Extrude menu to the screen (Figure 3.9).

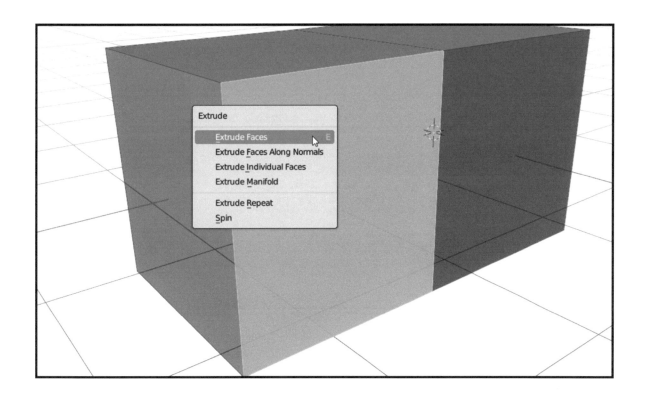

Figure 3.9 - Extrude menu

In some cases, you will also see the contextual menu that appears when you create objects in the 3D Viewport. You can change values for the offset (length) of your extrude (Figure 3.10).

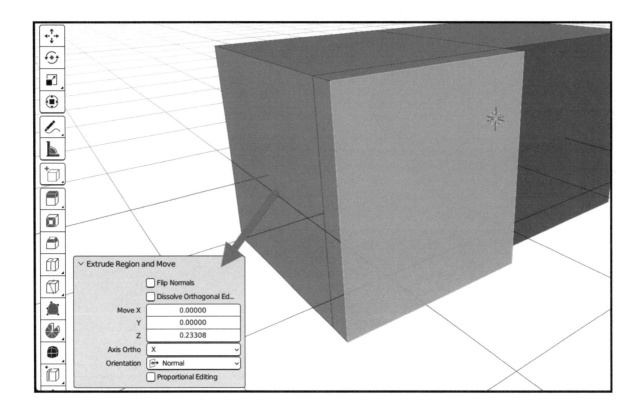

Figure 3.10 - *Contextual menu for extrudes*

Keep in mind that using the contextual menu is only possible right after you finish the extrude. It works the same way as with object creation. If you start another operation in Blender, you will no longer be able to change settings using that menu.

Tip: *The Toolbar options are also available in a floating menu that you can call using the SHIFT+SPACEBAR keys.*

116

3.3 Loop cut

The Loop cut tool is another useful option to change the shape of an existing object in Blender. Unlike the extrude tool, you won't create new geometry with the Loop cut. Instead, you add new edges to an existing model—the edges loop around your models' shape to give you more options in modeling.

To use a Loop cut, you can either use the CTRL+R keys in Edit Mode or the corresponding button from the Toolbar (Figure 3.11).

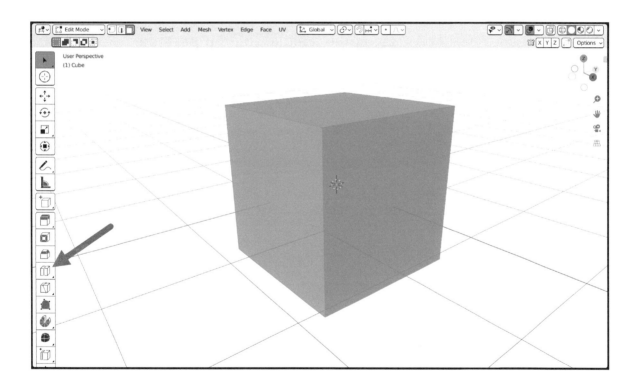

Figure 3.11 - *Loop cut button*

After pressing either the shortcut key or the button, you have to use a small sequence of clicks to create and align the Loop cut:

1. Move the mouse cursor over an edge. The cut will occur in a perpendicular direction from that edge.

2. Left-click once to confirm the direction of the cut

3. Move the cursor again to choose the location of your edge loop

4. Left-click again to set the location

5. To make your new Loop stay in the middle, you can press the ESC key instead of left-clicking

You can also create multiple cuts with the Loop cut when you are still selecting your new loops' direction. Before confirming the direction of your cuts with the first left-click, you can either use the mouse wheel or the plus and minus keys from your Numpad to create multiple cuts (Figure 3.12).

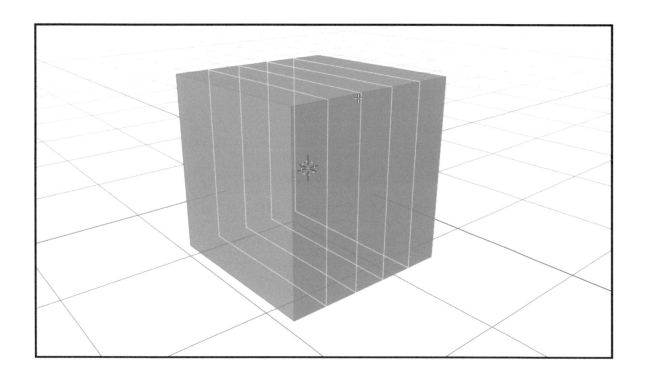

Figure 3.12 - *Multiple cuts*

That option to add multiple cuts only work if you trigger the Loop cut with their respective keyboard shortcut, which is CTRL+R.

After you add edge loops to the model, you can select the faces or any other element to apply an extrude. That gives you a lot of freedom regarding 3D modeling. It is possible to edit the number of cuts after adding them with the "Loop Cut and Slide" menu that appears on the lower right corner of the 3D Viewport. Use the "Number of Cuts" to edit your Loop cut.

3.3.1 Loop cut and Extrude Manifold

A powerful option introduced with Blender 2.9 is the Extrude Manifold that can erase and split faces based on extrudes. It works better for extrudes made to the interior of a model. You can see the real benefit of such extrude mode when pairing it with a Loop cut.

To see the benefits of such extrude, we can take an example from a simple cube that receives a horizontal segment with the Loop cut (Figure 3.13).

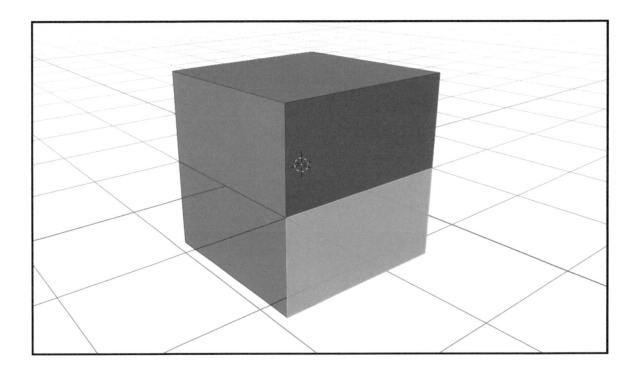

Figure 3.13 - *Cube with single cut*

In Figure 3.13, you can see a selected face where we apply both an Extrude Region and Manifold. The results are shown in Figure 3.14.

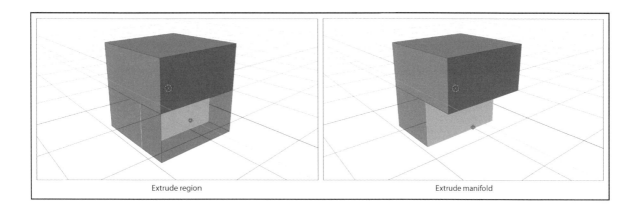

Figure 3.14 - *Comparing extrudes*

As you can see from the comparison, we got a face resulting from our Extrude Region going inward and keeping both sides. That will require the artist additional work to "fix" the geometry.

On the other hand, we have the Extrude Manifold managing to push the face inward and editing both sides simultaneously. That is a huge timesaver for 3D modeling.

3.4 Creating new edges and faces from vertices

There are some cases in 3D modeling where you might have two separate structures that you wish to connect. In Blender, we can connect objects using the F key when having two vertices or edges selected. The process is simple and only requires you to have at least two elements selected.

In Edit Mode, select two vertices in a model and press the F key to connect them with an edge (Figure 3.15).

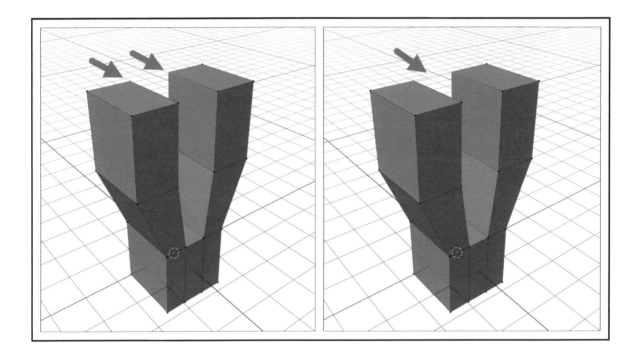

Figure 3.15 - Connecting vertices

You can also connect three and four vertices resulting in a face. Selecting three vertices also creates a new face. However, it is a common practice to avoid such types of faces. A triangular face usually breaks edge loops and won't create smooth deformations in animations.

If you have two edges selected, you can also press the F key to connect them with a face (Figure 3.16).

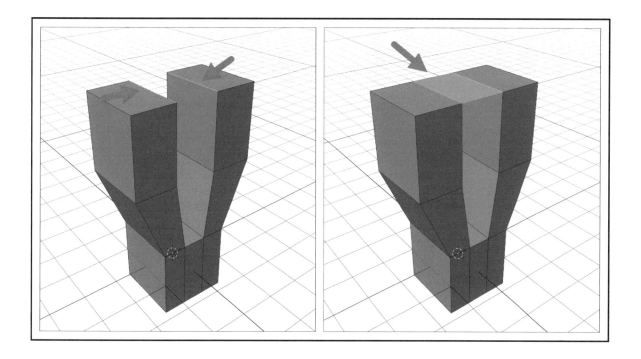

Figure 3.16 - *Connecting two edges*

The F key is a great tool to create new geometry based on connections of elements from a Mesh.

3.4.1 Connecting faces with the Bridge faces

The F key can connect the vertices and edges of a model, but won't work when the selected element is a face. To connect faces in a model, we have to use another tool.

For faces, we need the *Bridge Faces* that appears in the Context Menu. After selecting two faces, use a right-click to open that menu (Figure 3.17).

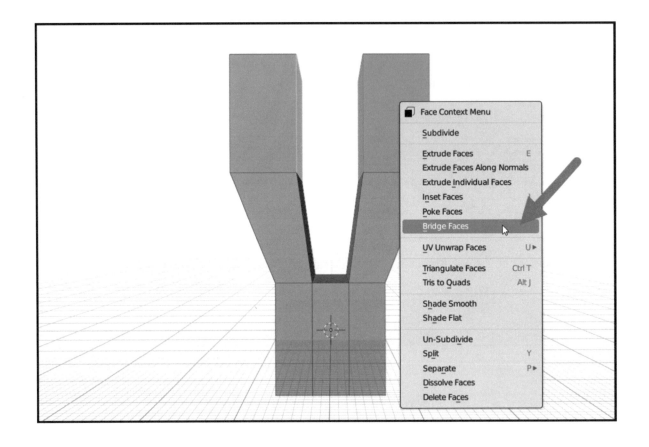

Figure 3.17 - Context menu

With the Bridge Faces, it is possible to connect two selected faces and create new geometry. You have to select the faces first and press the right mouse button. That opens the Context Menu. Pick Bridge Faces, and you get a connection between the two selected faces (Figure 3.18).

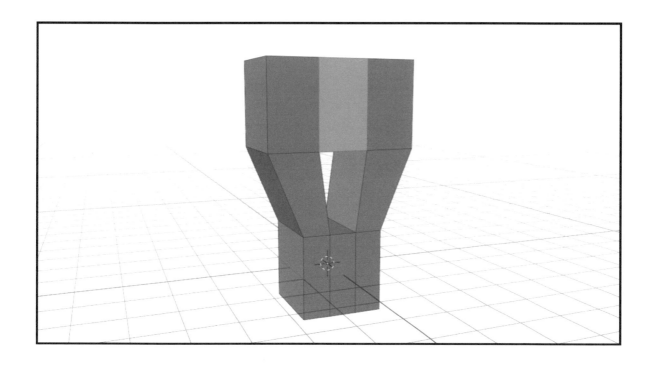

Figure 3.18 - *Connected faces*

The option will not work if you have more than two faces selected. With Bridge Faces, you get better results by using parallel faces. That is a way to avoid distorted shapes from the connected geometry.

3.5 Separating and joining models

In the previous section, we learned how to connect elements from a model with the F key and the Bridge Faces. What if we want to separate models instead of connecting them?

To separate parts of a model in Blender, use the P key. After pressing the P key, a small menu appears with options. It is possible to separate parts by selection, materials, and loose parts.

For instance, after pressing the P key and choosing "Selection," Blender creates a new object based on any selected vertices, edges, or faces. (Figure 3.19).

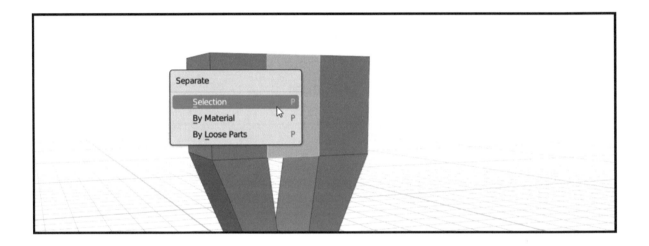

Figure 3.19 - *Separate option*

The separate option is useful for projects where you have to create derivate models from existing 3D objects. An isolated part could work as a starting point for new 3D models.

For example, look at the model shown in Figure 3.20.

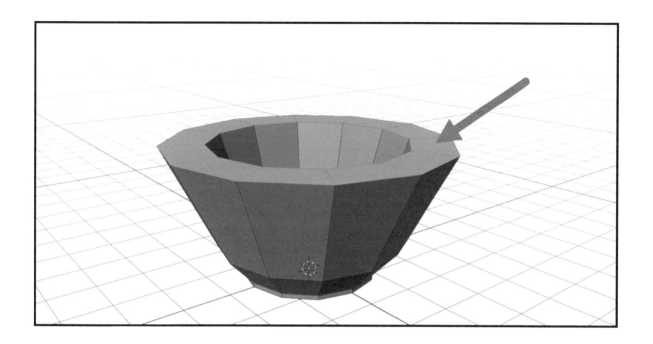

Figure 3.20 - *Model to separate*

The objective of this model is to start a derivate object using the faces pointed in Figure 3.20. It already has the correct size and scale. To start a new model based on that face, use the following workflow:

1. Select the faces

2. Press SHIFT+D to duplicate the faces

3. Press the ESC key to cancel the transformation of your duplicated faces

4. With the duplicated faces still selected, press the P key

5. Choose "Selection"

6. Switch to Object Mode

After switching to Object Mode, a new object based on those faces will be available for you to start modeling (Figure 3.21).

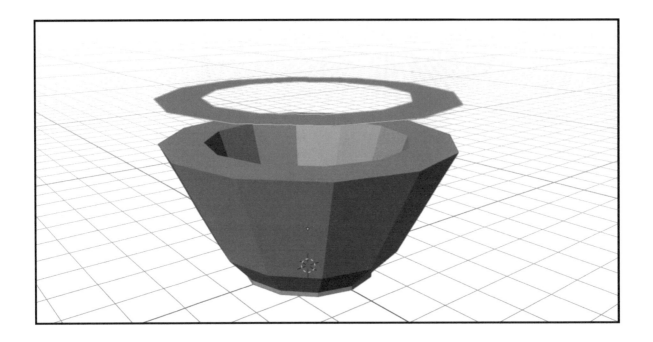

Figure 3.21 - New faces for modeling

If you cant select the new object, look at the Collections for a duplicate.

Part of the technique consists of canceling the transformation for the duplicated object with the ESC key. That creates the new objects in the same location from the initially selected faces. It also works for copies of edges and vertices. However, in Figure 3.21, the new object is in a higher Z coordinate to make it easier to visualize the outcome.

There is also an option in the **Mesh → Separate** menu to call the Separate options without the shortcut key.

Tip: Later you will also be able to separate objects by Material as it appears in the Separate options.

3.5.1 Joining models

After separating elements from a 3D model, you might want to turn them back into a single object. That requires an option to turn multiple individual objects into a unified entity. To merge two meshes in Blender, we can use the Join option. Select two or more objects and press the CTRL+J keys.

The join is also available in the **Object → Join** menu with multiple objects selected. Unlike the Separate option that required you to be in Edit Mode, you must trigger the Join option in Object Mode.

Using the Join option is useful when you want to connect parts of two different objects. The F key won't work on two separate objects, and also the Bridge Faces. With the Join tool, you can easily make a new object based on two or more shapes.

If you don't want to keep models as a single object, you can do all modeling tasks and separate them again with the P key.

3.6 Merging vertices

A typical modeling project in Blender might require a few hours of work using tools to extrude, connect, and cut models. That work results in a 3D object ready to receive materials and textures for rendering. It is possible to end up with duplicated vertices, edges, or faces in a particular region during the process.

That could create visual problems with modifiers like Subdivision Surface. In 3D modeling, those visual problems usually receive the name of "artifacts."

Luckily for us, we have a quick way to eliminate those duplicates using an option from the *Context Menu* called *Merge*. Using the Merge option, you can get two or more vertices from a model and turn them into a single vertex.

Info: The Merge options only appear when you have Vertex marked as the primary selection in Edit Mode.

For instance, if you look at Figure 3.22, you see a model with two vertices that we could merge.

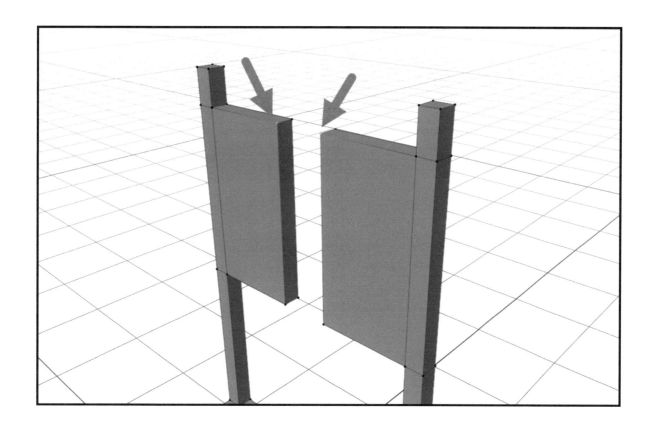

Figure 3.22 - *Vertices for Merge*

To use all options regarding merging, you can use the Context Menu in edit mode. Select the elements and right-click once (Figure 3.23).

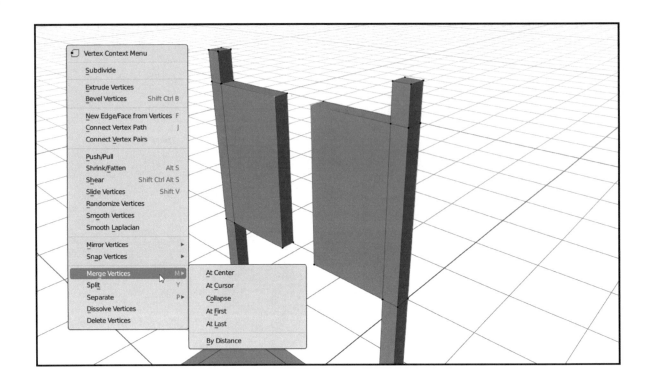

Figure 3.23 - Merge options

In the list, you will see the following options:

– **At First or At Last**: Use the first or last selected vertex.

– **At Center**: All vertices will merge using the median distance between all of them.

– **At Cursor**: The new vertice created will use the 3D Cursor location.

– **Collapse**: You will get islands of vertices merged based on the distance between them. Each island will merge into a new vertex.

– **By distance**: You will merge vertices based on the distance between them. For instance, using a length of zero will remove all duplicated vertices from a 3D model.

For the vertices from Figure 3.22, we can quickly fix the gap between those two vertices with a Merge based on the median distance. Select both vertices and with a right-click call the Context menu and pick **Merge** → **At Center** (Figure 3.24).

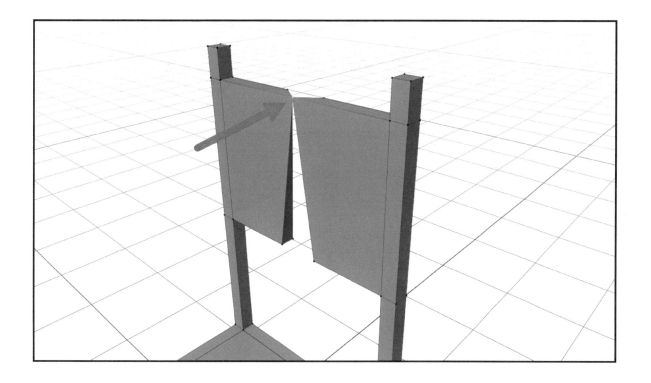

Figure 3.24 - *Merge results*

If you want to use a dedicated shortcut for the Merge, you can also press the M key with vertices selected. That will call a small menu with Merge options only.

Tip: *For the example in Figure 3.24, you can repeat the Merge to connect the other vertices.*

3.6.1 Fixing extrudes with the Merge

One of the uses for the Merge option in Blender is to fix problems created by the extrude, where you might forget to undo a canceled extrude during the transformation stage.

The problem appears when you press the E key to extrude and press the ESC key before finishing the extrude. That cancels the transformation, but the extrude's new elements will still exist in your scene.

By pressing CTRL+Z right after that operation, you remove those extra elements (vertices, edges, or faces). But, in case you forget to press CTRL+Z or use the **Edit →** **Undo** menu, all newly created elements will stay present until you start to see visual problems from modifiers and other operations.

You can easily fix that problem with a Merge using the distance option. Look at Figure 3.25 to see a model that had a canceled extrude for one of their faces.

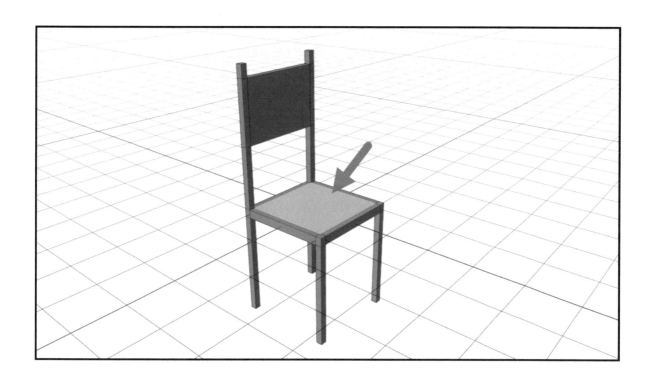

Figure 3.25 - *Model with duplicated vertices*

Visually, the model doesn't seem to have anything wrong with the polygon structure. But, if you select all vertices and press the M key (Merge) and choose the "By
Distance" option, you will see a message in the status bar of Blender pointing that it
removed four vertices (Figure 3.26).

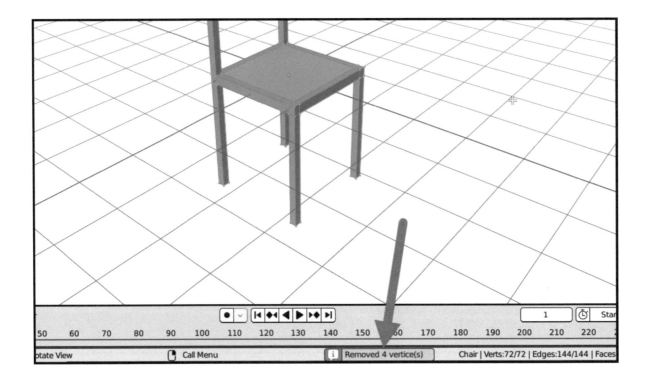

Figure 3.26 - Removed vertices

The downside of this procedure is that you will have to trigger the Merge option to remove duplicates manually.

But, an option from the Sidebar of Blender allows you to enable an *Auto Merge* option that automatically removes duplicates. Open the Sidebar with the N key and go to the Tools tab (Figure 3.27).

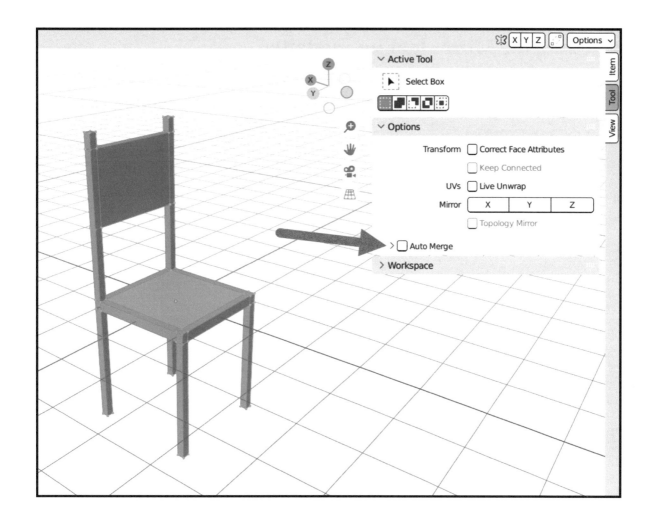

Figure 3.27 - Auto Merge option

With *Auto Merge* enabled, you can set the minimum distance used for merging polygon elements. The default distance (0.001) will make sure you have only vertices sharing the same location receiving an *Auto Merge*. Leave *Auto Merge* enabled to make Blender remove all those vertices without pressing the M key or the Context Menu.

3.7 Using the Mirror tool for modeling

A large number of objects that are subject to a 3D modeling in Blender will present some kind of symmetry. Working with any object with a symmetrical side makes your life a lot easier because we can create only half of the shape and mirror the other side.

In Blender, you have a few options to work with symmetrical models starting with the Mirror tool and going up until the Mirror Modifier used in Chapter 4.

The Mirror tool in Blender works with the CTRL+M key, which inverts any selected objects. You won't get a mirrored copy with the tool, but an inverted version of the model. For instance, we can take the model shown in Figure 3.28, representing only half of a 3D object.

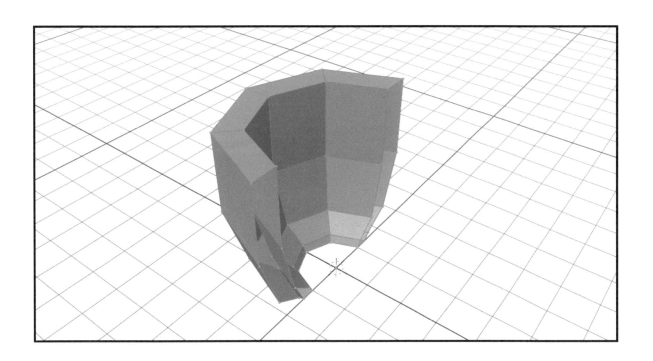

Figure 3.28 - *Half of a model*

If you go to Object Mode and press CTRL+M or use the **Object → Mirror** menu, you can invert the object shape. For the shortcut, you must press a key representing the axis in which the mirror will happen (Figure 3.29). Press the key corresponding to an axis after the CTRL+M.

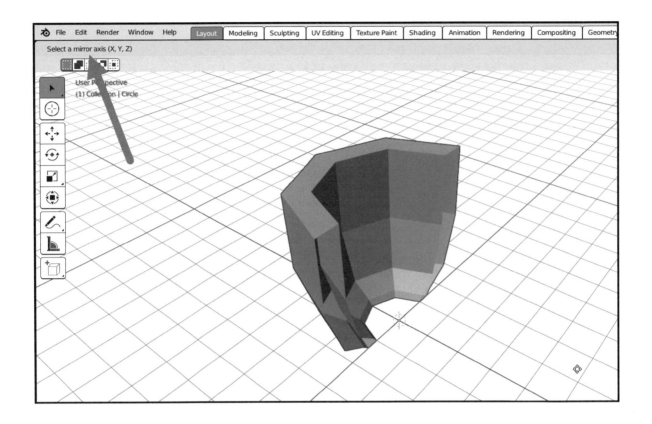

Figure 3.29 - *Mirror axis*

By choosing the **Object** → **Mirror** menu, you can pick the axis you want to use from the options list. The result will be a flipped version of the model. Using a SHIFT+D before you make the mirror, it is possible to create an inverted version of the model using a duplicate.

Using a move transformation with the flipped duplicate makes it possible to create a full model with a perfect symmetry (Figure 3.30).

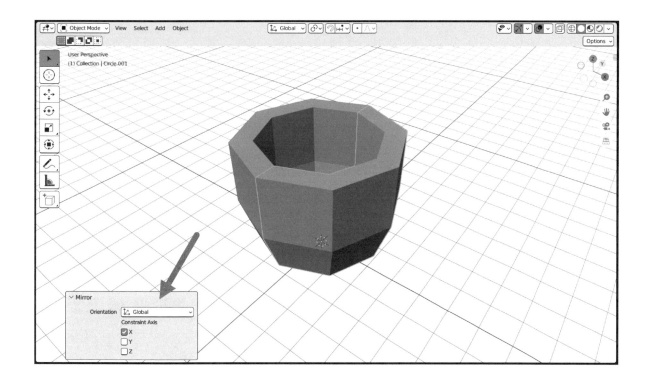

Figure 3.30 - *Full model with both sides*

Since they will be different objects, use a CTRL+J to join them, and later apply a Merge using the distance option. It removes all duplicated vertices.

Tip: *A trick used by some artists to apply a mirror using the Scale transformation consists of a scale with -100% of the object size. For instance, select the object and press the S key. Type -1 as the factor to get a mirror image of that model.*

141

What is next?

The extrude is an incredible tool and is by far one of the highlights of this chapter, but it won't solve all modeling challenges alone. You will still need additional tools to create complex models. But, in most projects, you use extrudes to build the vast majority of a model structure.

In the next chapter, we will learn how to use some of those tools in the modifiers section, where you will apply smoothing to 3D models and several replication modes to use patterns for modeling.

Besides modifies, you will also learn how to work with rounded profiles with the Spin tool, which will combine the use of an extrude with a rotation. That increases the number of options to create 3D models in Blender and give you more freedom to make complex objects.

Chapter 4 - Modeling techniques and resources

With the modeling tools from Blender, we can create a lot of different shapes and 3D objects for any project. There are multiple tools like modifiers, which can help in the creation of complex models. One of the most useful modifiers is the Subdivision Surface that can smooth polygons and help with organic modeling.

In this chapter, you will learn how to use modifiers and other options for modeling. Modifiers offer a wide range of options for 3D creation like smoothing, copying, and mirroring shapes. Besides modifiers, we will also learn how to manage tools like the Spin to create round shapes, which works like a mix of rotation and extrude.

If you follow the rules on using the Spin, you get unique shapes that wouldn't be possible with the extrude alone.

Here is a list of what you will learn:

– How to apply and manage modifiers

– Use the Subdivision surface modifier

– Control the smoothness of a Subdivision Surface

– Set the radius for the Subdivision Surface

– Apply different types of shading for models

– Use the Mirror modifier for symmetrical modeling

– Compose unique shapes with the Boolean

– Create models based on patterns with the Array

– Make round shapes with the Spin

– Use the proportional editing tools

4.1 Modifiers for modeling

In Blender, you will find a long list of tools and options regarding modeling that might help in multiple projects. Some of those options give you an extra level of flexibility in modeling tasks because they offer an easy way to enable and disable certain aspects of your workflow.

We are talking about modifiers. You find the modifiers at the Properties Editor in the Modifiers tab (Figure 4.1).

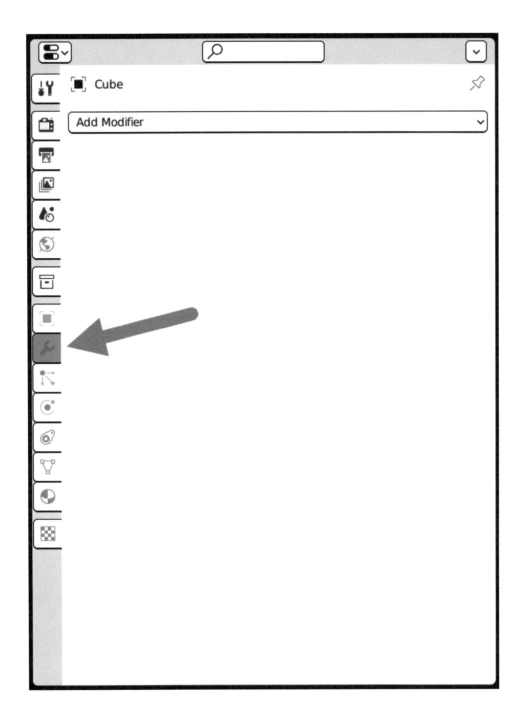

Figure 4.1 - *Modifiers for modeling*

Modifiers can help on multiple occasions and not only modeling, but we will start to work with them to transform some of our 3D objects. The first step to use a modifier is selecting an object to receive that "modification."

Use the "Add Modifier" option to pick one or more modifiers from the list. Once you add a modifier to an object, it appears in the Properties Editor at the Modifier tab (Figure 4.2).

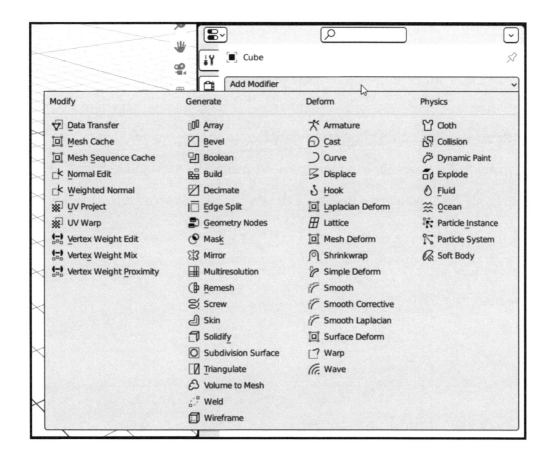

Figure 4.2 - Modifier list

A few aspects of modifiers that you should keep in mind:

– You can add as many modifiers to an object as you wish.

– The modifiers will stack on top of each other.

– Modifiers transform the model following the order in which they appear in the stack. Starting with the top modifier and following the order until the bottom.

– At any moment, you can reorder or remove a modifier from an object to exclude any modification made by that particular modifier.

Each modifier displays a few common controls to manage stack order, modifier duplication, make the modifier permanent, and more. To view all controls, you must press the small button (arrow pointing down) on the top right. In Figure 4.3, you can see a list of available controls.

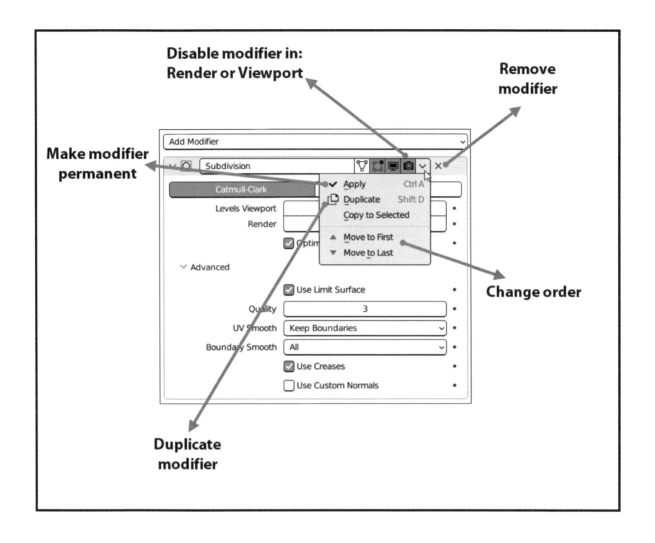

Figure 4.3 - Modifier controls

An important aspect of each modifier is that you will lose any effects it produces once you remove them from any object. If you want to make the effects permanent, use the "Apply" option available in each modifier. After using that option, the modifier disappears from the list, and the modification becomes part of the object.

That is useful when you have a project where you must create an object based on multiple modifiers, which you can also use as a reference to start modeling. For instance, it is possible to add a Mirror Modifier and make it a permanent part of a 3D model.

Tip: Before applying a modifier's effects, you should make a backup copy of your 3D model and place it to a different Collection. By hiding that Collection, you keep an untouched version of any 3D model with all modifiers.

4.2 Subdivision Surface modifier

One of the most used modifiers for modeling is the Subdivision Surface, which smoothes your 3D models by adding lots of new faces to the selected polygon. The modifier is one of the primary tools for techniques such as mesh modeling.

A popular workflow for many modeling projects is to start with a low poly version of an object, and later apply a modification to increase polygon count. By adding more polygons, it is also possible to smooth existing surfaces.

Figure 4.4 shows an example of the results of a Subdivision Surface Modifier (High Poly).

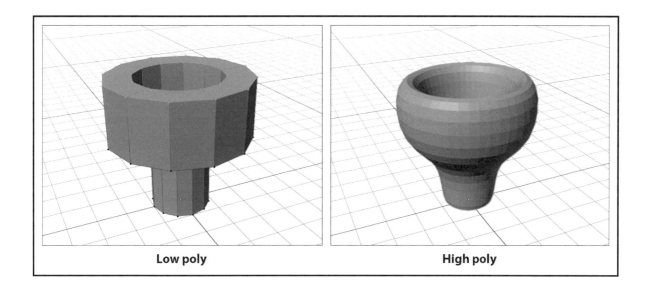

Figure 4.4 - *Smoothing 3D model*

To use that modifier, select the object you wish to smooth and pick Subdivision Surface from the modifier list. After assigning the modifier, it is possible to control smoothness from the modifier options (Figure 4.5).

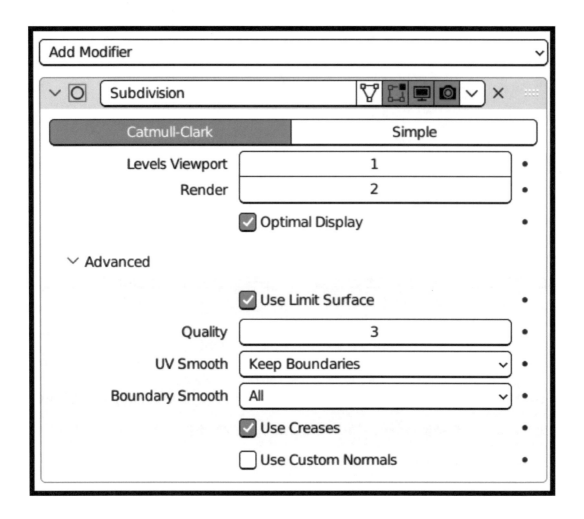

Figure 4.5 - Subdivision settings

What will determine the smoothness of your model is a combination of the subdivision count and algorithm. At the top, you will see two smoothing algorithms:

– **Catmull-Clark**: If you want a full smoothing of your model with rounded shapes, you should use this method.

– **Simple**: For projects where you want only new faces and divisions but no smoothing, you can use the simple option.

The level of subdivisions shows unique values for smoothing objects in the Viewport and Render. Usually, you will use a lower value for the Viewport and a higher level for the Render. The reason is that a model with a high level of subdivisions may add a significant computational load to your system.

With a high level or subdivisions, you might experience some common operations delays like changing the zoom and even swapping between Object and Edit Modes. Depending on the value and number of smoothed objects, you can even crash Blender.

A value of two for the 3D Viewport and three for Render usually shows great results for most 3D Models. Unless you have a project requiring more subdivisions, always use two for the viewport and three for render. In Figure 4.6, you can see the difference between using one and three for subdivisions.

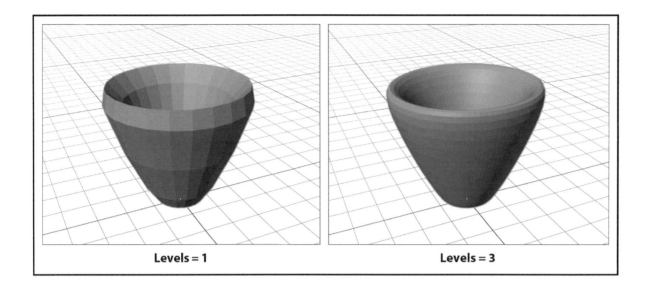

Figure 4.6 - *Different levels of subdivision*

With the Quality value, you can control the accuracy of how your modifier will place the vertices concerning the original object. Higher values will result in more precision locations but will add more computational load to the model.

4.2.1 Controlling surface smoothing

Even after using the Subdivision Surface modifier in a model, you might still see a few faces showing up. The modifier helps to create a smooth surface for the model, but won't remove visible borders from the faces it creates (Figure 4.7).

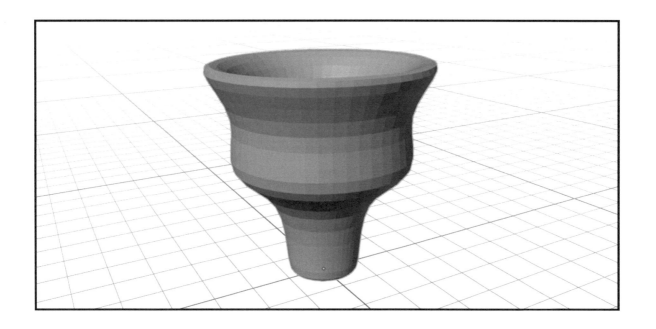

Figure 4.7 - *Face borders in objects*

To smooth the surface of any model, we have two shading options:

– Shade Smooth

– Shade Flat

By default, all models use Shade Flat, and in case you want to remove visible borders between polygons, change it to Shade Smooth. The option is available when you are in Object Mode. With an object selected, right-click to open the Context menu (Figure 4.8).

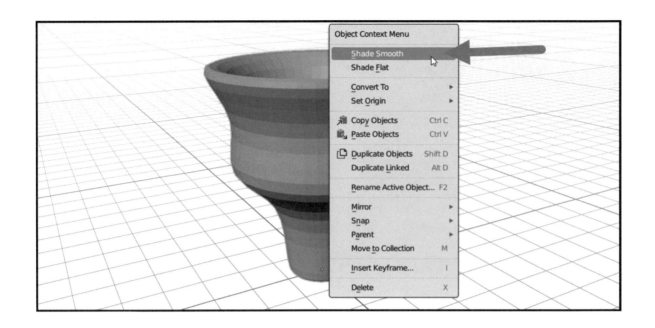

Figure 4.8 - Context menu

There you will see the Shading options, and by choosing Shade Smooth, you re-move the visible borders between each face (Figure 4.9).

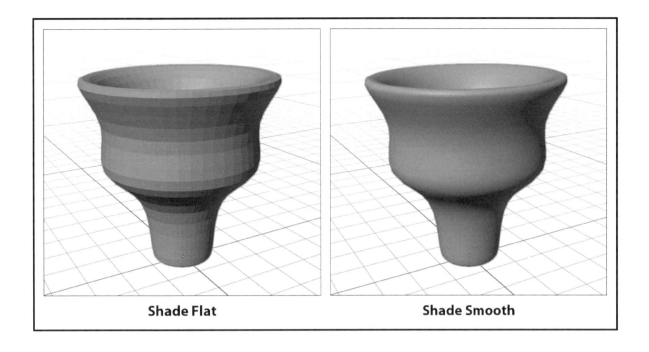

Shade Flat | **Shade Smooth**

Figure 4.9 - *Results of a Shade Smooth*

The option is also available at the **Object** Menu in Object Mode. After assigning a Subdivision Surface modifier to any object, you can enable Shade Smooth to make it have a surface with no visible borders between each face.

4.2.2 Fixing smoothing problems

In the process of smoothing 3D models, you might encounter a few problems caused by unmatched face normals. Face normals are the visible side of a 3D polygon, and depending on the tools and techniques applied to create each object, you may have normals facing in opposite directions.

For instance, if you look at the object in Figure 4.10, you see a dark spot from the smoothing process.

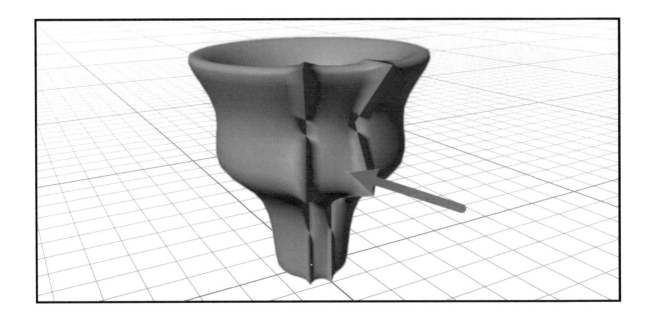

Figure 4.10 - *Object with dark spot*

To view the difference between normals in that object, we can enable the visualization of Face normals in the Overlays menu. That menu is available on the left of your shading options at the 3D Viewport header (Figure 4.11).

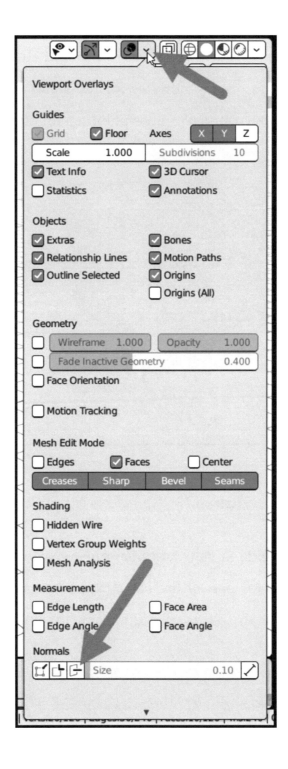

Figure 4.11 - Overlay options

Look to the lower side of your Overlays menu to find all options related to Normals. Enable the option to display normals for faces and increase their size. Your normals appear as small perpendicular lines pointing out of each face (Figure 4.12).

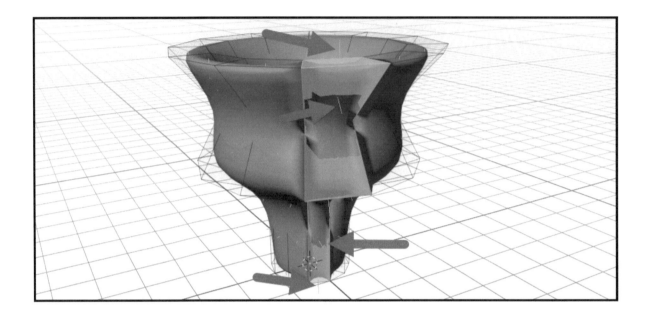

Figure 4.12 - *Normals in object*

You must be in Edit Mode to view and manipulate Normals as you can see from Figure 4.12, the normals for part of the object point in opposite directions. If you want a smooth surface for any object, all normals must point in the same direction.

Tip: At the overlays menu, you can also enable the Statistics option to display information about your modeling project on your 3D Viewport's top left. The Statistics option is in the top left.

You can force the recalculation of normals using the SHIFT+N keys to make Blender point all of them to the outside of a model. Before you press the keys, make sure you select all faces from the object with the A key. After selecting all faces, press SHIFT+N. The option is also available from the **Mesh → Normals → Recalculate Outside** menu.

As a result, you will get the faces pointing to the outside of the model and a clean, smooth surface (Figure 4.13).

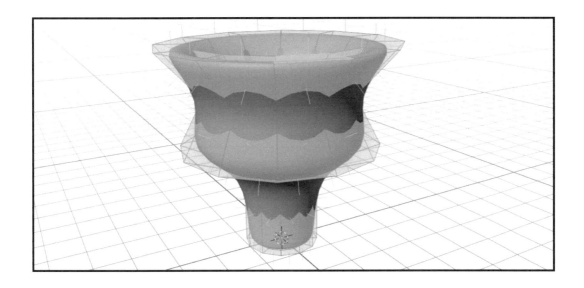

Figure 4.13 - *Clean smooth surface*

Whenever you see dark spots at an object surface after applying a Subdivision Surface modifier and a Shade Smooth, you probably have an issue with Face normals. Enable the display of Face normals in the Overlays menu to investigate and apply a fix.

You have additional options to handle normals in the **Mesh → Normals** menu.

Tip: If you want to invert the normals of a face you can use the Flip option from the Mesh → Normals menu.

4.2.3 Controlling smoothing radius with loops

Once you apply a Subdivision Surface modifier to an object, you will notice that it will round the edges and corners for those 3D models for some shapes. It is possible to control the roundness based on the distance between each edge of a mesh.

For instance, if you look at the model shown in Figure 4.14, you will see that it use a large relative radius for the smoothed version.

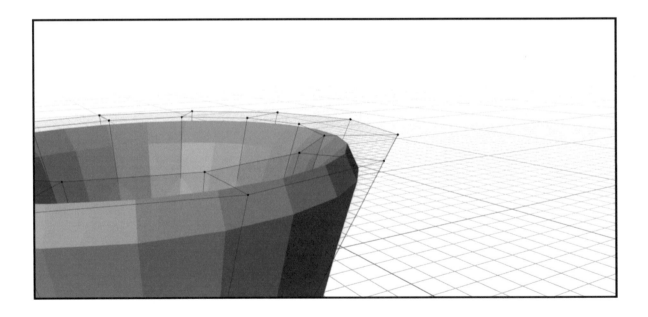

Figure 4.14 - Radius difference

You can control the smoothness radius with the Loop cut tool. By adding new edge loops close to the existing top edges, we can visually set the radius length. For instance, if we add a new loop near the top with the CTRL+R key and place it close to the upper edges (Figure 4.15).

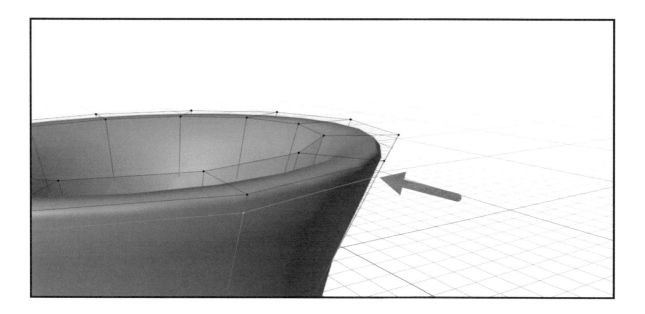

Figure 4.15 - *New loops results*

As a result, we get a smooth surface with e much smaller radius. You can use the Loop cut to add new edge loops and control every corner's sharpness whenever you have a model that receives a Subdivision Surface Modifier. Having two edge loops close to each other creates a sharper edge.

Tip: *You can easily select edge loops in Blender by holding the ALT key while selecting an edge. Blender will try to select all connected edges in a loop.*

4.3 Mirror modifier

In the modifiers list, you find another useful tool for modeling, which is the Mirror modifier. Unlike the Mirror tool that you can apply using the CTRL+M keys, you get a copy of your selected object using the Mirror modifier and not an inverted object.

To use the modifier, you must select the object you wish to mirror and assign the Mirror. You have to pick an axis from the settings to create the mirror copy (Figure 4.16).

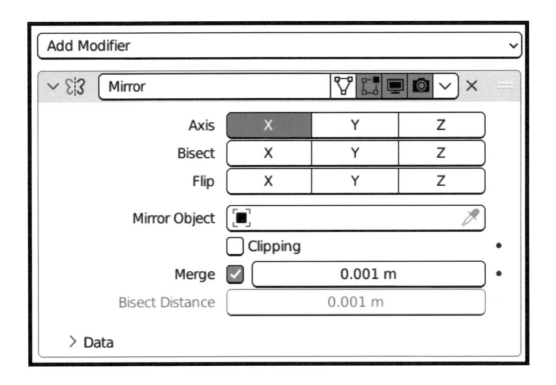

Figure 4.16 - *Mirror modifier*

Choose the axis, and you get a mirrored copy of your object with the origin point as the pivot for the new object location (Figure 4.17).

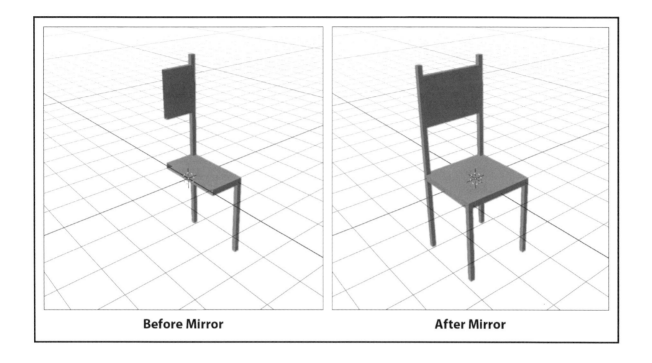

Before Mirror   After Mirror

Figure 4.17 - *Mirror results*

The location of your origin point is the main reference to place your mirrored copy. In Figure 4.16, the origin point is at the left side of our object. If the origin point was in a distant location from the object, your copies would also appear with the same distance.

The origin point works as a pivot point. It uses the same base distance from any source object.

After adding a Mirror modifier to any object, you can make that copy and source model become a single object using the Apply option. That removes the modifier from the list and join both objects. Look to the Merge Limit option, at the Mirror settings, to set a minimum distance used to merge vertices from the two sides.

In some cases, your workflow requires other modifiers to create a more complex 3D model. The order in which you add a modifier could impact the final result. For instance, in Figure 4.18, you can see an object that receives a Mirror first and then a Subdivision Surface.

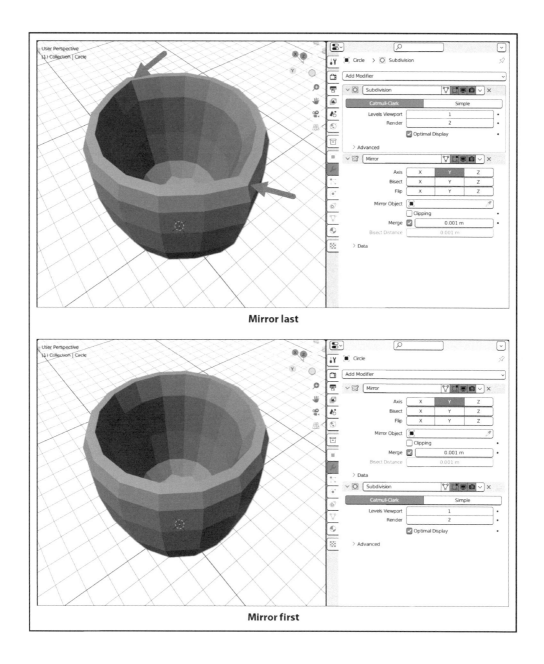

Mirror last

Mirror first

Figure 4.18 - *Modifiers order*

Notice how the model with a mirror as the first modifier displays a much better 3D topology showing a regular and round shape.

It will first have a mirrored copy and then a smoothed surface. Always consider the order in which you will use modifiers to change the surface of an object. In any case, you can change the order of the modifiers by clicking and dragging each modifier from the list. Use the small dots on the top right corner of each modifier.

4.4 Array modifier

If you have a shape formed by smaller objects organized in a matrix style, you can use an Array modifier to create such a model. With the Array, we can get any object copied in multiple axes.

For instance, if we use the form shown in Figure 4.19 and apply an Array Modifier. You get several copies of that shape repeated side by side.

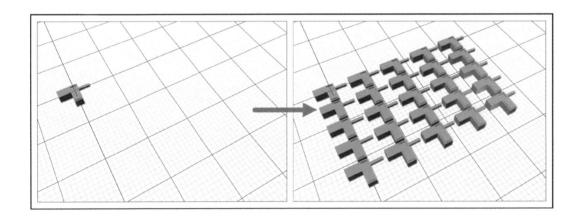

Figure 4.19 - *Shape with Array*

To use an Array for modeling, select the object first, and add the modifier. Once you have the Array modifier assigned, change the settings to start making copies of the object (Figure 4.20).

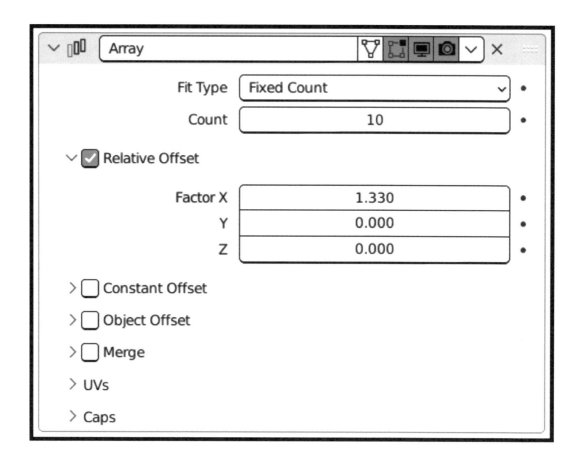

Figure 4.20 - Array options

At the top, you have the Count that controls the number of copies. There are three main types of methods available for duplicating models:

– **Fixed count**: Uses a relative size for the selected object. For instance, in the distance, you will enter the value two, and it will use two times the size of your object as a distance.

– **Fit length**: Here, you get absolute distances. If you use a value of 2, the copies will stay at two units from each other regardless of the object size.

– **Fit Curve**: You can also use a curve object to control the size. You can create a curve with the SHIFT+A keys and choose the Curve group.

After choosing the method you want to use, it is time to pick the values and axis used to place each duplicate. For instance, in the X field, you can set the value used for copies in the X-axis. If you use a value of 1 for the X and 3 for Count, you will get five copies on the X-axis.

Using the Fixed Count type, they will repeat three times in the X-axis (Figure 4.21).

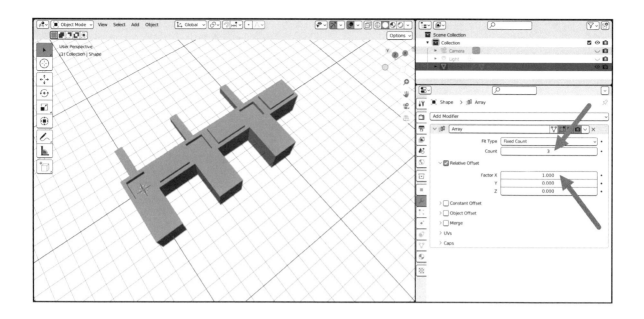

Figure 4.21 - Copies in the X-axis

Using those same values makes three copies with a distance of one unit in the X-axis if you choose Fit Length.

A single Array Modifier will only make copies in either a row or column of objects. You need two Arrays to get a bi-dimensional pattern (rows and columns). For instance, we can use one Array for the X-axis and other for the Y-axis (Figure 4.22).

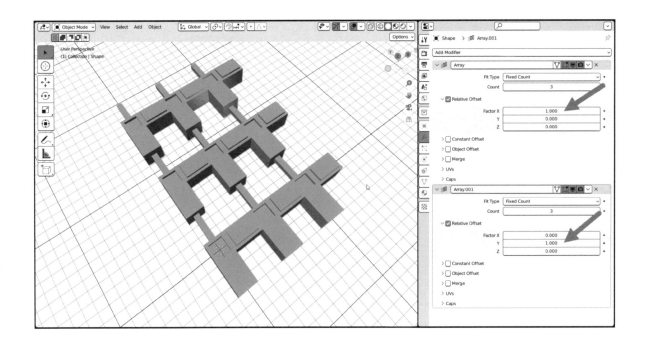

Figure 4.22 - Copies with two Arrays

That is the easiest way to get a matrix style set of copies.

4.4.1 Arrays and reference objects

Besides using values to control an Array's distance, you can also use an object to set ranges and even rotations for any Array. It could be an existing 3d Model from your scene or a helper object like an Empty from Blender.

An Empty is a unique type of object in Blender that will not appear during rendering. It works only as a helper for modeling, animation, or any other task that requires a reference object.

172

You can create an Empty using the SHIFT+A key and choose Empty with the option *Plain Axis* for the most straightforward Empty (Figure 4.23).

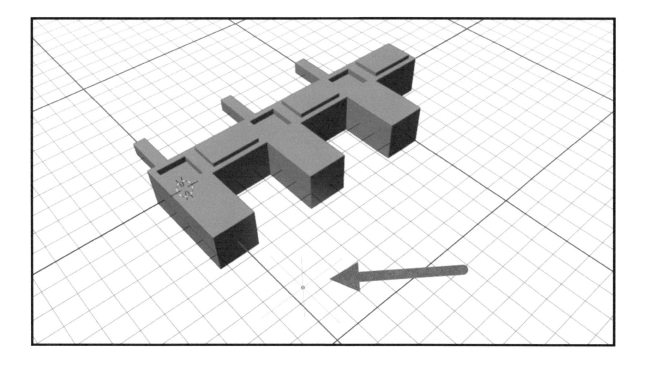

Figure 4.23 - *Empty object*

How can an Empty help us with an Array? At the Array options, you have a field called Object Offset. Use the Empty as the Object Offset.

We can use any object from the scene in Blender as the Object Offset, which controls distance, rotation, and scaling. The Empty is convenient for offering an invisible reference object. It won't appear in a render.

For instance, if you have an existing Array and add an Empty to the Object Offset field, it will immediately control your Array. If you rotate and move the Empty, it creates a unique shape using the Array (Figure 4.24).

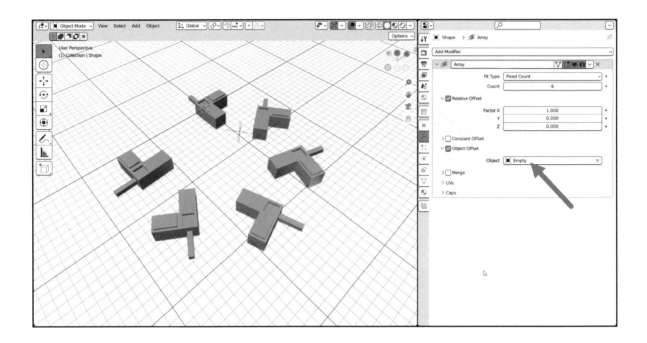

Figure 4.24 - Array with Empty

Once you enable the Object Offset in the Array options, use the text field or eye-dropper to pick an object by name. Choose the name for the Empty, which will probably be "Empty."

If you add some animation data to the Empty, it can generate some interesting abstract animations using the Array. You will learn more about animation with Blender in chapter 7.

Tip: *Remember that you can easily rename any object in your project using the F2 key. Select the object and press the key to assign a new name.*

4.5 Boolean modifier

Another useful modifier for 3D modeling is the Boolean, which allows you to create models based on interactions between objects. The modifier creates new shapes based on:

– Intersections

– Subtractions

– Unions

The 3D objects created from those interactions would be difficult to create using "traditional" modeling techniques. For most of the operations, you need at least two objects, which you have to select by name. As a reminder, you can easily set unique names for objects with the F2 key.

One of the most typical uses of the Boolean Modifier is to open round holes in 3D objects. For that task, you need an object to modify and a cylinder. Place the cylinder at the same location where you want to open the hole (Figure 4.25).

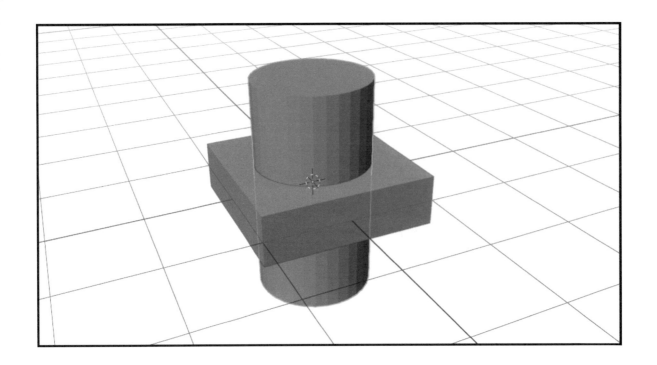

Figure 4.25 - *Objects for Boolean*

After placing both objects, assign the Boolean modifier to the object that should receive the hole. Set the Operation as Difference to subtract the shape from another object. Add the cylinder as the second object pointing it by his name at the Object field (Figure 4.26).

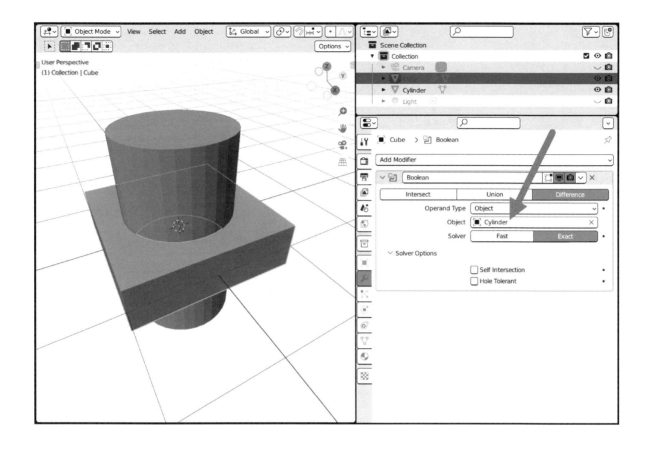

Figure 4.26 - *Boolean settings*

At first, you won't notice any changes to either object, because the Boolean apply the modification in real-time. You must use the Apply option to make the change permanent, and after moving the base object, you see the hole with the same shape of your cylinder (Figure 4.27).

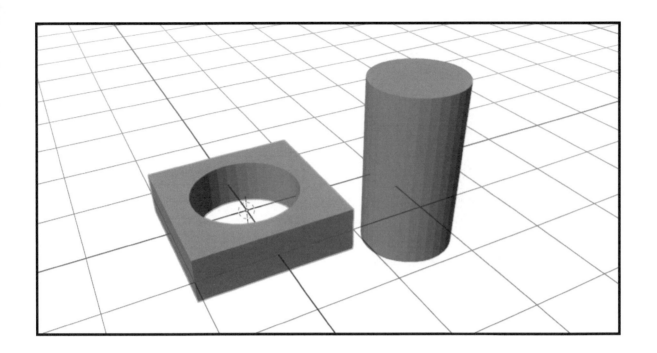

Figure 4.27 - *Boolean results*

The Union option creates a new shape based on the merge of two existing objects, and with the Intersect, you will get a new shape based on the shared space between two 3D models.

4.6 Spin tool for rounded shapes

For the cases where you need parts of a model to have a perfectly rounded shape, it will be hard to use only a combination of extrudes and Subdivision Surfaces. In Blender, we have a tool called Spin that can help to create perfectly rounded shapes. The Spin works like an extrude that follows a circular path.

As a result, you get an arch shape for the selected object. Using the Spin is easy if you follow a few rules to create each shape:

– The Spin uses the 3D Cursor as the pivot point for the rotation and arch center.

– You must activate the Spin with a perpendicular view from your rotation plane.

– Use the small menu on the lower left of your 3D Viewport to control the segmentation and angle for the Spin.

– Control the direction of the Spin with positive or negative values for the Angle value at the Spin options.

In Figure 4.28, you can see an example of what you can create using the Spin.

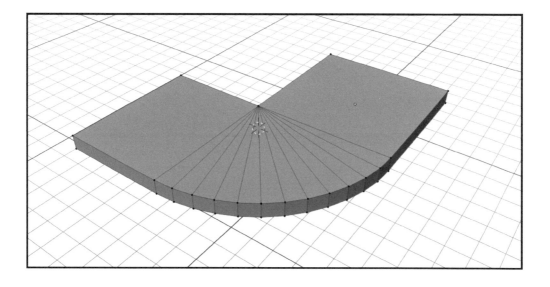

Figure 4.28 - *Rounded shape from the Spin*

To use the Spin, you have to go into Edit Mode and select your model's parts to replicate with the Spin. For instance, we can select the face from a shape like the one shown in Figure 4.29.

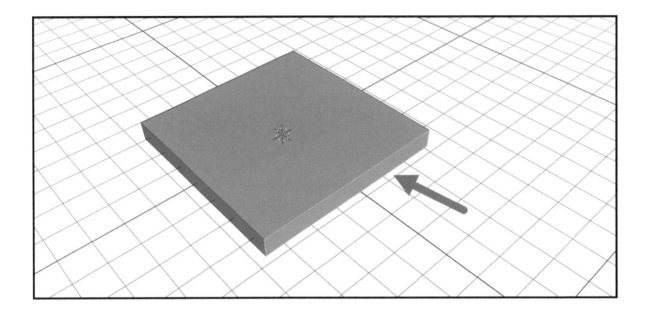

Figure 4.29 - *Face for the Spin*

Once you have the selected elements, which could also be a set of edges or vertices, you must place the 3D Cursor. Move the 3D Cursor location to the point you wish to use as the pivot in your Spin rotation (Figure 4.30).

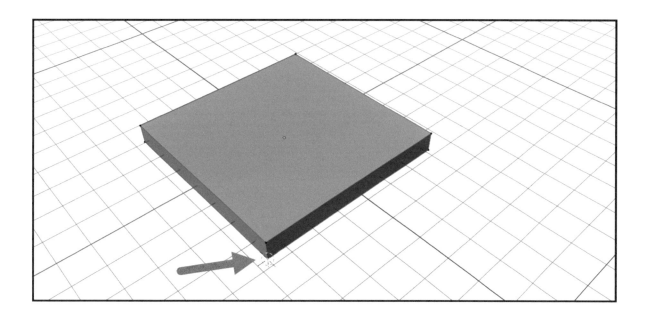

Figure 4.30 - *3D Cursor location*

The easiest way to move your 3D Cursor to that location is by using the Snap tool (SHIFT+S). Before you trigger the Spin from the Toolbar of your 3D Viewport, you must set your view from the object to the top. Press the seven key on your Numpad.

Always consider the plane where your Spin will occur. The view you have must be perpendicular to that plane. In our case, the Spin happens in the X and Y-axis plane. For that reason, using the Top view is the best option.

What happens if you don't change the view? The Spin will use any perpendicular projected plane, based on your current viewing angle.

When in the top view, press the Spin button. A blue arc appears close to the selected elements. Click and drag your mouse above the arch, and you start to see your round shape appearing. At the Spin options on the lower-left corner, you can control the rounded shape's rotation and steps (Figure 4.31).

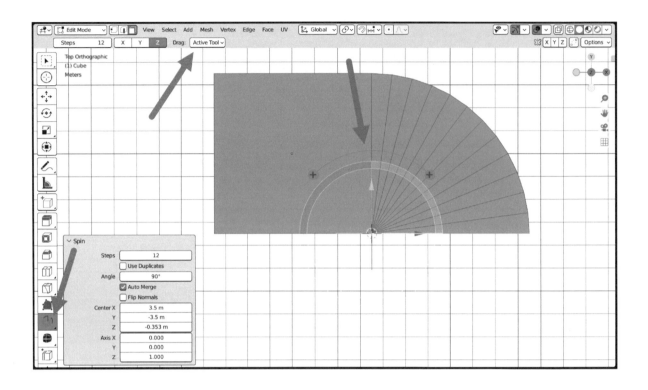

Figure 4.31 - Spin shape

Make sure you get all the options and settings for the Spin right after you make the Spin because the menu disappears after you start another operation in Blender.

In the Spin menu, you find an option called "Use Duplicates" that doesn't connect the Spin's copies. It works like a rotation based Array.

4.7 Proportional editing

The transformations we apply to any polygon elements in Blender take full effect on selected elements; they will not influence anything at their surroundings if not selected. For instance, if you choose a couple of vertices from a polygon with hundreds of vertices and press the S key, it will apply a scale only to the selected vertices.

What if you also wanted to apply transformations to surrounding vertices with a lower influence? You can do that with the Proportional Editing tools. The option is available at the 3D Viewport header, and you can also enable it with the O key (Figure 4.32).

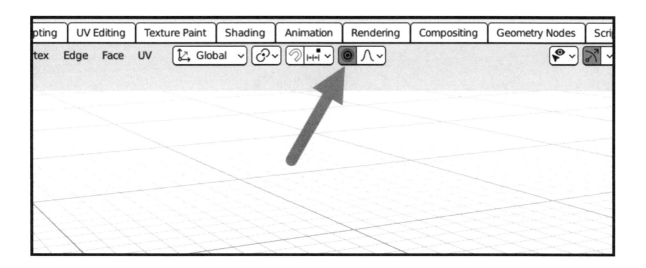

Figure 4.32 - Proportional editing tools

After enabling the Proportional Editing, you must choose a falloff type from the options right next to the icon where you trigger the Proportional Editing tools (Figure 4.33).

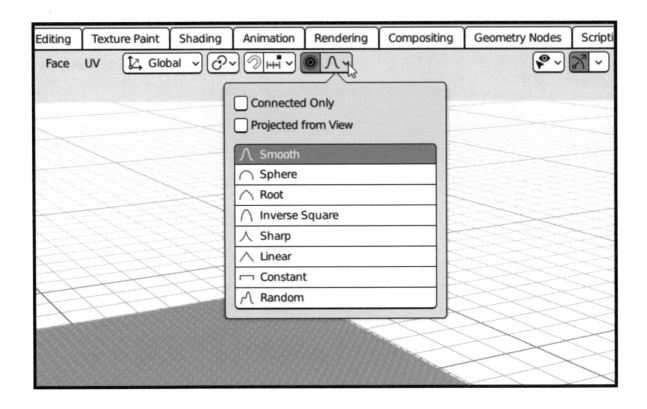

Figure 4.33 - *Fallout types*

By enabling a Proportional Editing and using as fallout type the smoothing option, you can select a single vertex from a plane with multiple subdivisions. Start a move transformation in the Z-axis with the G key and Z key. As a result, you will get the surrounding vertices also moving up (Figure 4.34).

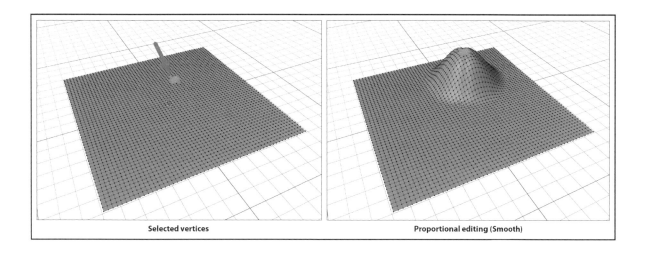

Figure 4.34 - *Proportional editing vertices*

You will notice that a small circle appears around the selected vertex, while it is transforming, showing the area of influence for the Proportional Editing. It is possible to increase or decrease the influence using your mouse wheel or the plus and minus keys from your Numpad.

You can create a plane like the one shown in Figure 4.34 with the Context menu:

1. Select the plane and go to Edit Mode.

2. In Edit Mode, press the A key to select all vertices and with a right-click open the Context menu.

3. There you will choose the first option called Subdivision.

For each time you choose the Subdivision, you will get the edges of a model divided once. Apply multiple of those Subdivisions to get a high-density mesh.

What is next?

The next step to improve or projects in Blender is applying materials and textures to the objects. Using materials, we can give a visual context to 3D models and greatly increase a scene's realism. In Blender, you will find several controls that will allow you to create realistic materials.

You will learn how to apply and manage materials for rendering in the next chapter. We will learn how to use textures that work in both Eevee and Cycles.

From simple materials that use a standard shader, we jump straight to PBR materials that use a mix from multiple textures to create realistic surfaces. You will learn all the tools required to start making materials for your projects.

Chapter 5 - Materials and textures

Using materials and textures is a crucial component for any project, and this chapter has all the information you need to manage and apply materials or textures to objects. You will find two main editors in Blender to handle materials: Material tab (Properties Editor) and Shader Editor. The Shader Editor helps us using Nodes for materials.

The Nodes gives you a lot of flexibility and power to craft all kinds of materials, using a visual workflow. Using materials based on multiple texture maps, you will be ready to create realistic images using Blender. Those have the name of PBR materials.

You will also learn how to use and find some high-quality PBR materials for your projects.

Here is a list of what you will learn:

– Apply materials to objects

– Manage and rename materials

– Protect materials from the purge process with a Fake user

– Choose the best shader for a material

– Use image textures

– Control projection and tilling for textures

– Apply PBR materials to objects

– Use Nodes to control and craft materials

– Apply glossy and transparent shaders to objects

– Use multiple materials for the same object

5.1 Adding materials to objects

Any scene in Blender can benefit from a combination of good lighting and realistic materials. With the materials tab, you have plenty of tools and options to assign shaders, textures, and other effects to give visual context for surfaces.

For instance, if you have to create a 3D model that should appear as a stone wall, you can use a texture on that object to make it look like a stone wall. We can create all types of surfaces based on a combination of shaders, effects, and textures.

Before we start to handle material creation and shaders, it is essential to define a few aspects of materials in Blender:

- A material must have one or multiple objects assigned.

- You can remove a material from an object. If a material doesn't have any assigned objects, Blender will purge that material when you save and close the project file.

- Multiple objects can use the same material.

- Each material must receive a unique name that will help you identify what it represents visually.

– You can reuse materials in other projects using the Append or Link options from the File menu.

To create a Blender material, you have to select an object first and then go to the Material tab at the Properties Editor (Figure 5.1).

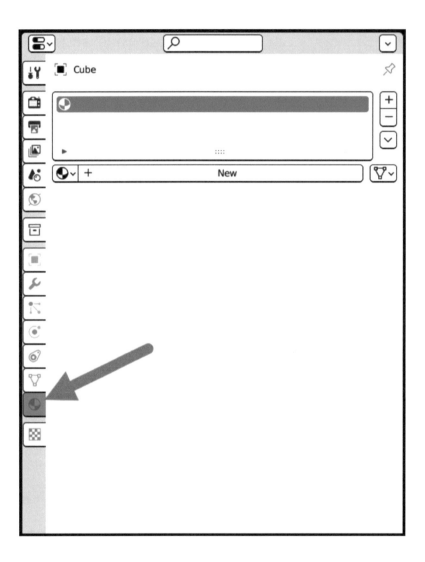

Figure 5.1 - *Material tab*

You will either see a button that allows you to create a new material or a list with options to edit any existing materials assigned to the selected 3D model at the Material tab.

For objects that already have a material, you see multiple controls available to manage the material at the top (Figure 5.2).

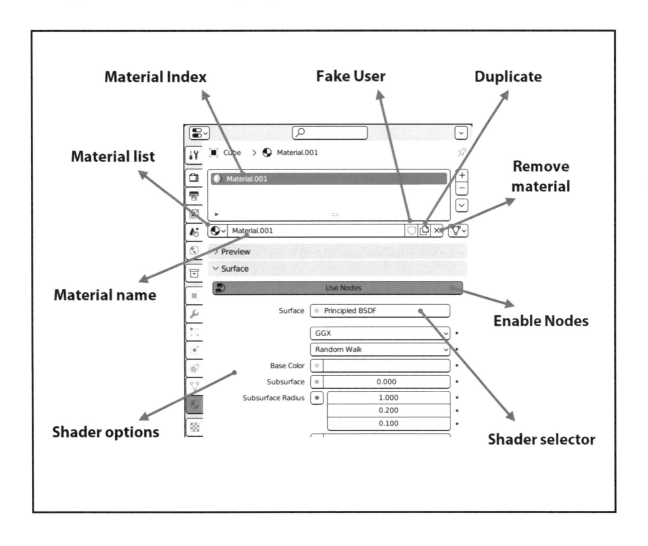

Figure 5.2 - Material controls

Here is a list with what you can do with each of the controls:

– **Material Name**: In the text field, you can rename the material. It is important to assign meaningful names for materials, which will help you later identify what they represent.

– **Remove**: With this button, you can remove the material from the object. It won't erase the material. If it doesn't have any objects assigned, Blender will purge the material the next time you exit the software.

– **Duplicate**: In some cases, you may want to create a new material using another one as a template. With the duplicate button, you can create a copy of the existing material.

– **Fake user**: Any material that doesn't have an object assigned will be at risk of deletion when you close Blender. You can enable the Fake User to keep any material from getting purged, even if it doesn't have any objects assigned.

– **Enable Nodes:** Makes all information from a material to appear at the Shader Editor using Nodes. Later in this chapter, we will learn how to use Nodes.

– **Material list**: All your materials will become part of the Blender file you are working at the moment. Using this button lists all materials available in this file, and you can easily reuse any of them. Instead of creating new materials, you can select an object and pick one from this list. The list is also useful to show materials that don't have any objects assigned. You will see a zero right next to a material that doesn't have any objects assigned.

- **Material index**: We can have multiple materials in a single object using index-es. Here you have a list of all materials assigned for each index in the object.

- **Shader selector:** Each material can use different shaders, and you can select one from a list in this selector.

- **Shader options:** Depending on the selected shader, you might see different options to set up their visual properties.

Using these controls makes the management of materials a lot easier and allow re-use.

Info: *Many of the materials options work with the same settings regardless of the render-er you choose. That is the case for Cycles and Eevee.*

5.2 Materials and shaders

After you create a material, the first thing you have to do is choose a proper shader. A shader is one of the most important elements of any material because it controls how the object interacts with light. For instance, you can have a material that be-haves like glass or an opaque surface.

What sets the look of any material is the shader you choose from a list of available options (Figure 5.3). Look for the Surface option at the Material tab.

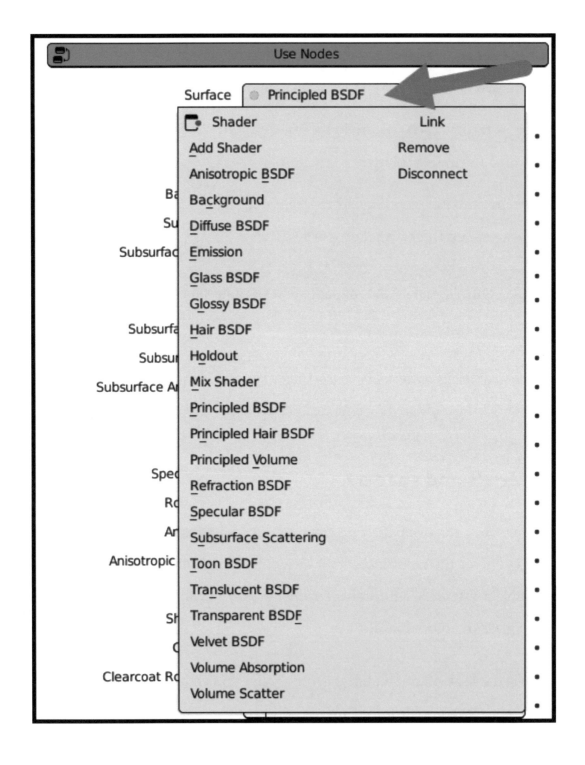

Figure 5.3 - *Shader list for Blender*

From the list you will find some shaders like:

– **Diffuse BSDF**: A simple shader that will create an opaque surface absorbing all light.

– **Glossy BSDF**: The shader you will want to use for surfaces that have any reflection level like mirrors and some types of metals.

– **Glass BSDF**: If you need realistic transparency, you will use the Glass BSDF for advanced reflections and light distortion.

– **Emission**: A material that will behave like a light source and contribute to a scene's lighting.

– **Mix Shader**: With this option, you can blend multiple shaders to create unique effects.

– **Transparent BSDF**: If you need simple transparency in materials, you will use the Transparent BSDF.

– **Principled BSDF**: A powerful shader that can create most of the effects alone and be the base for all surfaces using physically-based materials.

On the top right, you have the Remove and Disconnect. The first option excludes information from the current shader and places an empty "none" as the selection. With the Disconnect, you keep most of the settings but lose the shader's connection with the material. It will still be available from your Shader Editor.

Info: *The disconnect keeps the existing shader as a Node, which you can use from the Shader Editor.*

To use any of the shaders, you will have to select them from the list shown in Figure 5.3. Once you pick a shader, it will be time to set up all details about the surface. Some shaders offer simple controls like the Diffuse BSDF that lets you set a color for the material.

Others like the Principled BSDF feature a full list of settings that we will discuss in more detail at section *5.4 PBR texture in Blender.*

Info: *The BSDF acronym means Bidirectional Scattering Distribution Function, which identifies the mathematical function that controls how a surface scatter light.*

If you have to create materials with only a simple color, add the Diffuse BSDF as a shader. That shader has a color picker, and you will be able to get the color you want and use it for any selected 3D object (Figure 5.4).

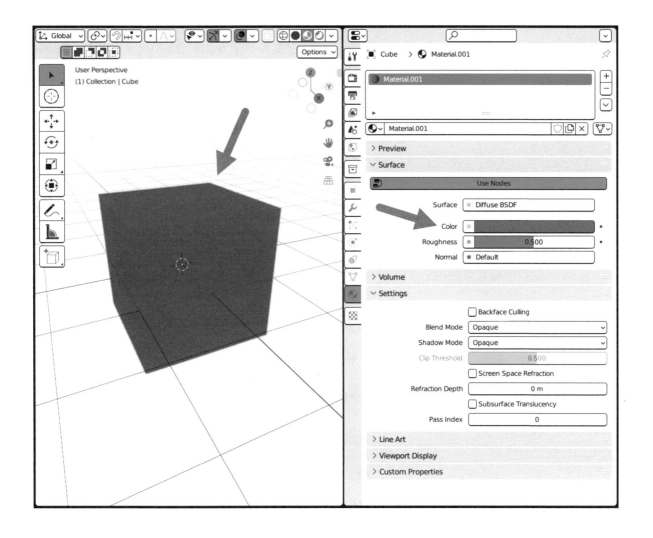

Figure 5.4 - *Diffuse BSDF material*

Notice how each field in the material options has a colored circle on the left side. Those circles and colors identify the type of data you can use for each field. A green circle means a shader, and a yellow one means color. The grey and blue represent numeric values and height information, respectively.

Regarding material previews, you can view how the material looks in two locations:

1. At the Material tab, you will see a Preview field that will display the materials in a geometrical primitive.

2. You can also use the 3D Viewport by choosing either the Rendered or Material Preview shading mode. Press the Z key and choose Rendered. For real-time previews, make sure you are using Eevee for rendering. That is the default renderer for Blender. Even if you swap for Cycles later, you can use Eevee for fast material previews.

The Material tab shows all the important options in a vertical list of settings. However, you can also use the Shader Editor for much better flexibility in material creation.

5.2.1 The Shader Editor

The Material tab gives us many options to craft and design materials for any 3D object, but when it is time to create complex surfaces and mix multiple options, we need something more advanced. One of the only ways to get that flexibility is with the Shader Editor.

That is a special type of Editor in Blender that displays data in a workflow style using Nodes for data like Shaders. A Node is a small box that collects information about a function, effect, shader, etc. With the Shader Editor, you have options to edit not only materials but also your environment and even post-processing effects for rendering.

To open the Shader Editor, you can either use a WorkSpace for shading or swap an existing division in your interface with the Shader Editor. For instance, you can use the Timeline area from the default user interface and open a Shader Editor (Figure 5.5).

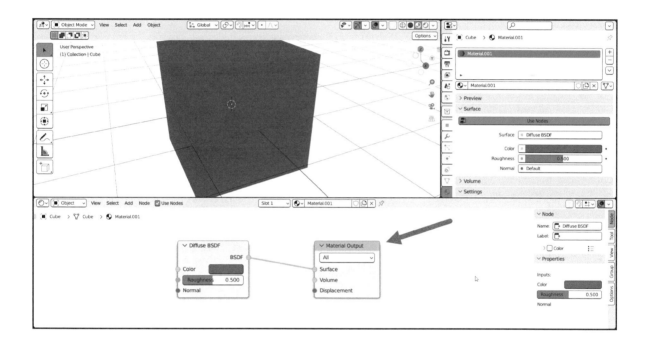

Figure 5.5 - Shader Editor

With the Shader Editor, you will see blocks of information for materials that receive the name of Node. You connect Nodes like a workflow of information from left to right. For materials, you always have the last Node on a chain as the "Material Output," and what comes before this Node will depend on the material you create.

A few important facts about Nodes:

– Each Node could have input and output sockets that are those circles on the side of each Node. For instance, you will see Shaders having both input and output. The "Material Output" Node only has input sockets.

– The sockets have color codes that identify what type of data they can handle. The colors are the same ones from the Material tab.

– You can connect Nodes by clicking and dragging from an output socket to an input.

– To select and manipulate Nodes, you can use the same shortcuts from the 3D Viewport.

– You can hold the CTRL key to break a connection while clicking and dragging with the right mouse button. The cursor will turn to a knife, and you will be able to cut connections.

– You can erase a Node with either the X key or DEL.

– To create new Nodes, you can use the SHIFT+A key or the Add menu in the Shader Editor.

A simple example of what we can do with the Shader Editor is with the Mix Shader that will allow us to blend two different shaders for a single material. We can mix a Diffuse BSDF and a Glossy BSDF:

1. Select an object and add a new material.

2. Choose the Diffuse BSDF as the Shader.

3. Open the Shader Editor

4. Press the SHIFT+A keys, and from the Shaders group add a Mix Shader

5. Press the SHIFT+A again, and from the Shaders group add a Glossy BSDF

You will get the Nodes shown in Figure 5.6.

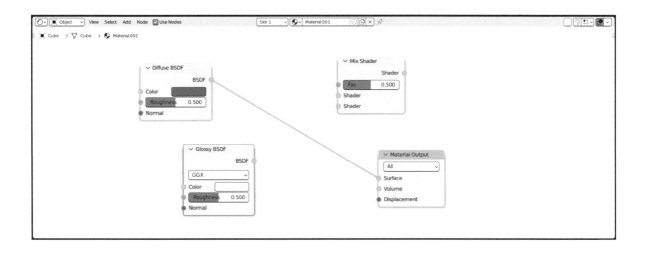

Figure 5.6 - *Nodes with no connections*

Now, we have to rearrange the Nodes to make both the Diffuse BSDF and Glossy BSDF connect to the Mix Shader. The Mix Shader connects to the Material Output.

To connect Nodes, we have two options:

– You can break the connection from the Diffuse BSDF to the Material Output by holding the CTRL key while clicking and dragging with the right mouse button. Click and drag from the output sockets of the Diffuse and Glossy to the Mix Shader. Connect the Mix Shader to the Material Output.

– Since the Diffuse BSDF already has a connection to the Material Output, move the Mix Shader Node until it is above the connection line between the Diffuse BSDF and Material Output. You will see the line becoming highlighted, and if you release the Mix Shader, it rearranges the connections and stay between both Nodes. You can connect the Glossy BSDF to the Mix Shader once the Diffuse has a connection.

Both options produce the same result, which you can see in Figure 5.7.

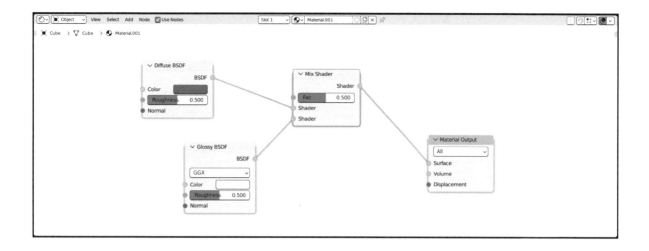

Figure 5.7 - *Material results with the Mix Shader*

The handling of all other Nodes and materials uses similar settings and procedures. By the way, you can do the same thing with the Material tab. From the Shaders settings, you can choose the Mix Shader (Figure 5.8).

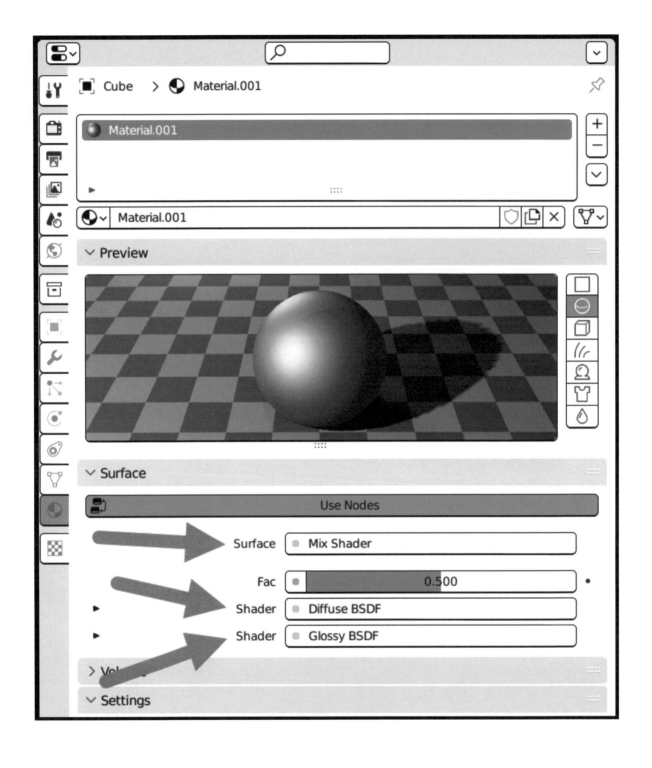

Figure 5.8 - Mix Shader

In the Mix Shader, you can select the two different Shaders that compose a material. You have the option to use either the Material tab or Shader Editor. The advantage of using the Shader Editor is that it works more visually and gives you an edge when using complex materials with multiple Nodes.

By adding another Mix Shader to any of the slots, you can blend even more Nodes in a material. The same applies to the Shader Editor, where you can add more Mix Shader Nodes or duplicate an existing Node with the SHIFT+D keys to compose more complex materials.

5.3 Using image textures

Using the Shaders alone won't produce realistic results for some surfaces, where an image texture is the best choice. To add an image texture to any material, use a Node called "Image Texture."

Info: From this point forward, we will use mainly the Shader Editor to craft materials. But, you will get the same results with the Material tab.

To add the Node to the material, press the SHIFT+A key, or use the Add menu in the Shader Editor. Go to the Texture group and choose Image Texture (Figure 5.9).

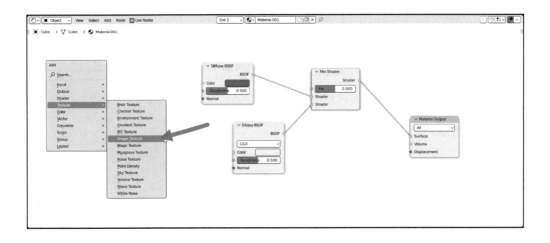

Figure 5.9 - Image Texture

You will click on the "Open" button to pick an image file from your hard drive or a local network from the Node. After opening a texture file, connect the Texture Node to the input socket of your Diffuse BSDF (Figure 5.10).

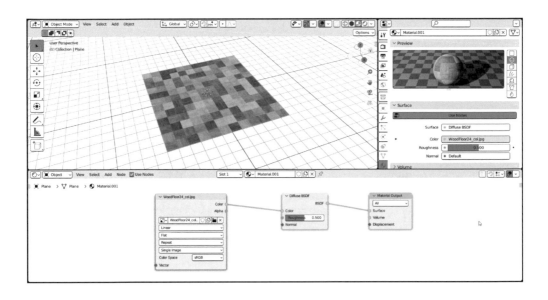

Figure 5.10 - Image Texture

The result will be a texture assigned to the material. Any Shader with an input socket receiving color data (Yellow) will connect with the Image Texture Node.

5.3.1 Projection for image textures

Each image you use in a material has an option for the projection type, which affects how it appears in any 3D object. The projection options are available at the Image Texture Node, and by default, will always start as "Flat." That means your image will look good on bidimensional surfaces like planes (Figure 5.11).

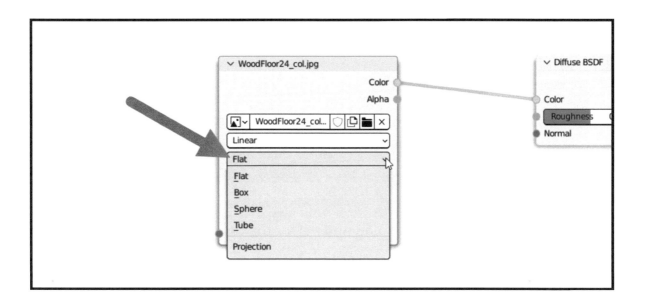

Figure 5.11 - Projection options

However, using "Flat" in shapes that also have a depth might result in distortions. You can choose other types of projections that can match the shape of multiple objects. A common choice for 3D models with textures is the "Box" that will consider an object as a whole (Figure 5.12).

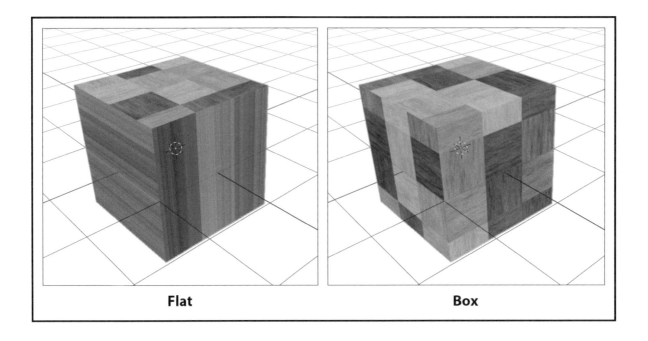

Figure 5.12 - *Box projection*

You can use the other two mapping options for the cases where you have a spherical or cylindrical 3D model; Sphere or Cylinder.

5.3.2 Tilling for image textures

After having a texture assigned to any material, you probably want to have additional controls for certain visual aspects of that image. One of those aspects is the distribution of an image at any 3D model surface. Usually, you want a texture with a repeating pattern that can cover a large surface. The technique has a name of tilling.

Unless you add controls to generate that tilling effect, image-based textures will not repeat on a surface. Instead, all images stretch to fit all available area of a surface. To create a tilling effect, you will need two additional Nodes:

– From the Input → **Texture Coordinates**

– From the Vector → **Mapping**

Connect the Generated output socket from the Texture Coordinates to the Mapping. From the Mapping, you will connect it to the Image Texture (Figure 5.13).

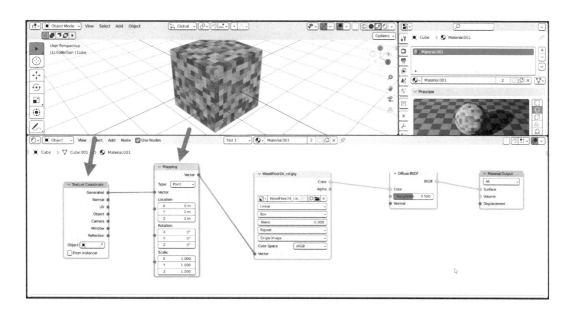

Figure 5.13 - *Tilling controls*

To control the tilling of textures, we use the Scale field from the Mapping Node. If you increase the size for the scale, the Mapping multiplies the textures in the same region, for instance, by using a scale of two for all axis in a Cube, result in two textures side by side in all axis (Figure 5.14).

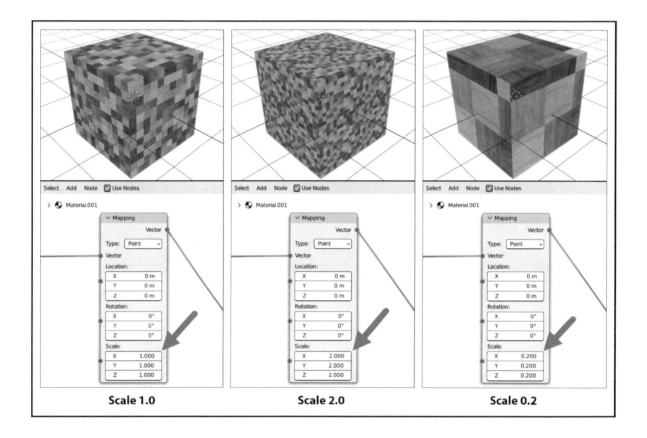

Figure 5.14 - Texture tilling

If you want to increase your textures' size, use smaller values like "0.5" that will cut in half the size of your textures.

Tip: *To use textures with tilling, you should always look for seamless texture images. Those textures won't show visible borders when placed side by side.*

5.4 PBR textures in Blender

For projects where you need maximum realism for materials, you must use a special type of PBR material. The acronym means "Physically Based Render" and identifies a material that has multiple textures. Each texture in the material has a unique purpose of representing a feature of the surface.

Usually, a simple PBR material feature texture maps for:

– Color (Diffuse)

– Roughness

– Normal (Bump)

You must connect each map to the corresponding input socket of a Shader, to produce a realistic material. The best Shader for PBR materials is the Principled BSDF (Figure 5.15).

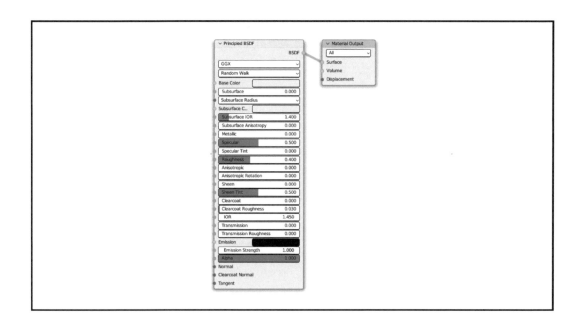

Figure 5.15 - *Principled BSDF*

Before we start using PBR materials, you have to find some of those special sets of textures. A PBR material usually comes with multiple of those maps available. Several online libraries offer free PBR materials. Some of the best sources for PBR materials:

– ambientcg.com

– texturehaven.com

– cgbookcase.com

They provide high-quality PBR textures in the public domain with resolutions going up to 8k (8.192 pixels):

- **1K**: 1024 x 1024 pixels

- **2K**: 2048 x 2048 pixels

- **4K**: 4096 x 4096 pixels

- **8K**: 8192 x 8192 pixels

Usually, textures in the PBR format feature a square size proportion for all images. That helps with the tiling process of those textures. Most of them are seamless. You can place them side by side with no visible borders.

You can download most of those textures as a compacted zip file. After extracting those files to your hard drive, you will get multiple image files with a suffix identifying the map (Figure 5.16).

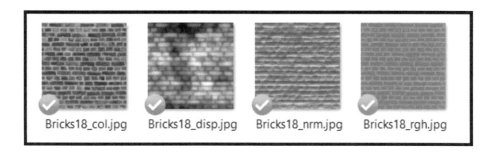

Figure 5.16 - *PBR material files*

The naming pattern for each texture map may change based on your textures' source, but they will most likely follow the same types of surfaces.

To set up a PBR material, create a new material, and choose the Principled BSDF as a shader. Add an Image Texture Node by pressing the SHIFT+A key in the Shader Editor. You can also drag and drop the image file from your file manager to the Shader Editor.

Dragging image files to the Shader Editor makes Blender automatically create an Image Texture Node with that image as the source.

For the remaining Image Texture Nodes, you can select the first Texture Node and press SHIFT+D twice. It creates two copies of the Image Texture Node. Or drag and drop the remaining image textures to the Shader Editor (Figure 5.17).

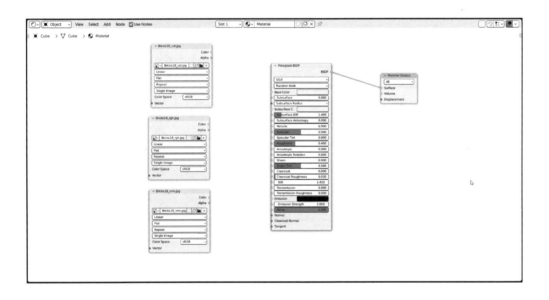

Figure 5.17 - Image Textures

For this example, we are using a PBR material with a Normal map. The Normal and Roughness maps don't affect colors, and for that reason, you should change the color space settings to "Non-Color" (Figure 5.18).

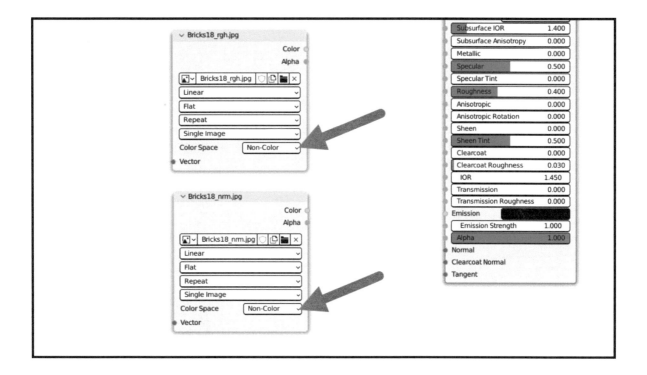

Figure 5.18 - Color Settings

After setting the Color Space, we can start connecting the Image Texture Nodes to the Principled BSDF:

1. Connect the Color textures to the Base Color

2. Connect the Roughness texture to the Roughness

For the Normal Texture, we need an additional Node, which you can create from the Vector group. Press SHIFT+A and add a Normal Map Node:

1. Connect the Normal texture to the Normal Map

2. Connect the Normal Map to the Normal

At the end of the process, you should have a Node setup like Figure 5.19 shows.

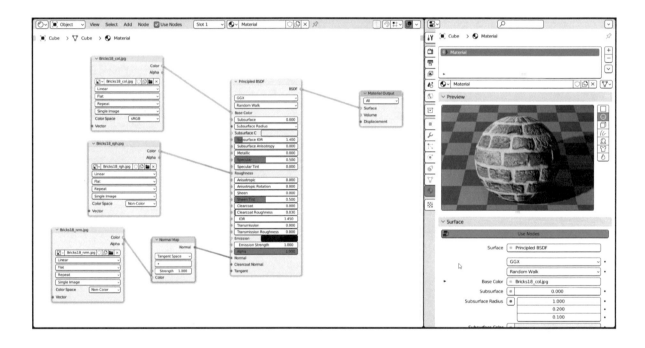

Figure 5.19 - *PBR material with maps*

With the Normal Map Node, it is possible to control the direction of your Bump. For instance, using negative values will invert the ridges created by the map. Change the Strength value to control the height of a normal map.

You can also add tilling control to the PBR material with the Texture Coordinate and Mapping. Connect the Mapping to each one of the Image Textures for full control (Figure 5.20).

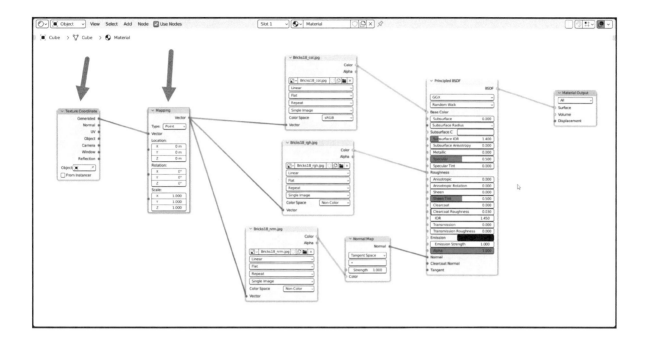

Figure 5.20 - *Tilling control*

In some textures, you will also find additional maps like Displacement and AO (Ambient Occlusion). Those maps connect with specific input sockets for the Principled BSDF.

The Ambient Occlusion connects to the Base Color, where you will need to use a MixRGB Node from the Color group to blend it with the color map (Figure 5.21). For the MixRGB, use the Multiply option.

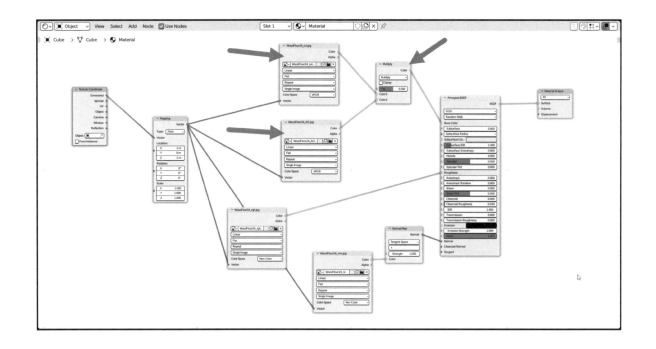

Figure 5.21 - *Ambient Occlusion map*

Most of the PBR materials offer the same types of maps regarding textures. It is a matter of following the same pattern with Image Texture Nodes and a Principled BSDF. You will be able to create dozens of PBR materials easily. To save time during this process, it is even possible to design a template with a material that has all Nodes ready, but no actual texture files selected.

Duplicate that "blank" material and assign all texture files to start a new PBR set-up. It can save a couple of minutes every time you have to put together a new material.

Tip: *It is also possible to "import" materials from other files in Blender. Use the* ***File*** *→* ***Append*** *or* ***File*** *→* ***Link*** *options to incorporate or reference existing materials. Select a*

218

Blender file and navigate to the "Materials" folder. Select the materials you wish to use and reuse them in any new projects.

5.5 Transparent and glass materials

For materials that require transparency, you can use options like the Glass BSDF and Transparency BSDF. With the Transparency BSDF, you will get materials with a simple effect that doesn't divert light (Figure 5.22).

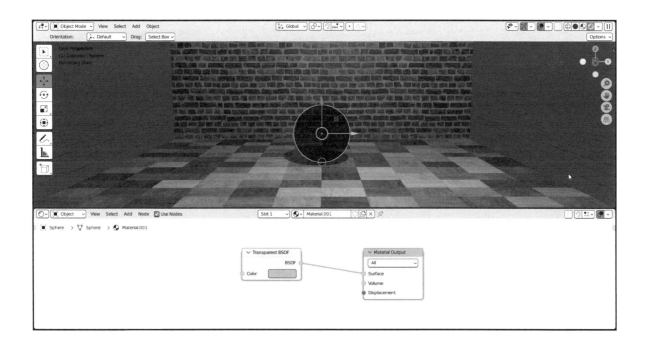

Figure 5.22 - Transparent BSDF (Cycles)

In case you need more sophisticated transparency, you should pick the Glass BSDF. The shader has two settings that will help you achieve a more realistic effect:

– **IOR**: An index that controls the refraction of light.

– **Roughness**: Here, you can control the smoothness of your surface reflection. Values close to zero will create a polish glass surface, and higher values will make it look grainy.

A material with the Glass BSDF can produce realistic results with advanced transparency (Figure 5.23).

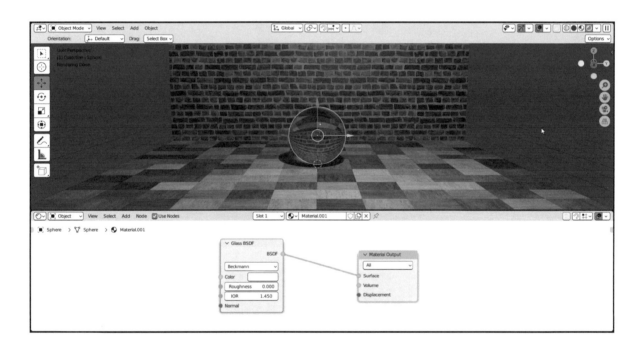

Figure 5.23 - Glass BSDF (Cycles)

Use the IOR settings to control how the light diverts from your model's interior using a material with a Glass BSDF. You can also mix shaders to achieve unique effects using transparency.

220

5.6 Glossy surfaces

If you want a surface with a certain level of reflection, you must use either a Glossy BSDF or the Principled BSDF. Both shaders feature settings that control how your material will reflect light: *roughness*.

A material that has a roughness close to zero has a perfect reflection, almost like a mirror. For higher values, it starts to get a blurred reflection until you can't identify the objects reflected anymore (Figure 5.24).

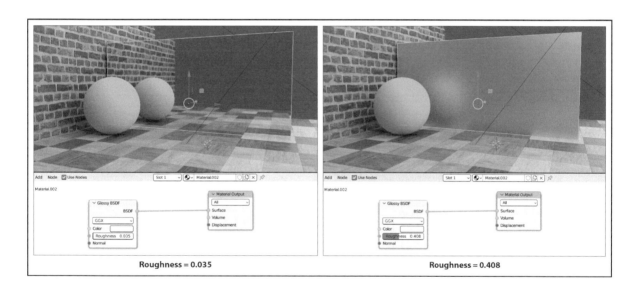

Figure 5.24 - Glossy surfaces

If you want a perfect mirror in a material, set the Roughness to zero and the color from the Glossy BSDF color as black.

5.7 Attaching textures to the Blender file

Any image-based texture added to materials in Blender is an external resource for your main project file. It is possible to manage and handle those files independently from Blender. If you backup the Blender project file alone, it won't have any of the image texture files used for materials, unless you merge them in a single file.

For instance, if you want to copy Blender project files to an external hard drive or sent it to a cloud drive, all texture files must follow the Blender file to the same location. Usually, it is a good practice to place those files in the same folder. That way, you can backup and copy the entire folder at once.

After adding textures to a material, they will either have a relative or absolute path to the Blender file. Following the folder recommendation for Blender files, you should always create a unique folder for your project. In that folder, save the Blender file alongside all additional resources like textures.

It makes handling external data easier for large projects, especially if you have to move the project file somewhere else.

An easy way to avoid all that trouble is to attach your external files to the Blender project file. You can do that with the **File → External Data** menu (Figure 5.25).

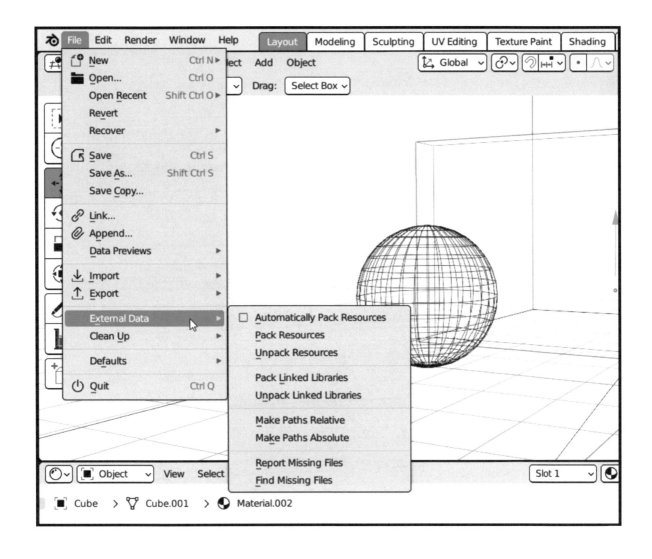

Figure 5.25 - External data options

Using an option called "Pack All Into .blend" attaches all external resources to the Blender project file, making both Blender files and image textures a single file. They will work as if they were a ZIP file that has multiple files inside.

__Info__: An external file that has a path starting with "// "has a relative path and will most likely come from the same folder of your project file.

After using that option, you won't have to worry about external files anymore because all textures are now part of your project file. However, it may significantly increase the size of your project file. If you have a project file with 1MB in size and 300MB of textures, the new project file size will be 301MB.

As a way to automate the packing of external data, you can enable the "Automatically Pack All Into .blend." Use the "Unpack All Into Files" to extract the files to your project folder.

There is also an option to unpack texture files right next to the image filename individually. At the Image Texture Node, you will see a button called Unpack Item (Figure 5.26).

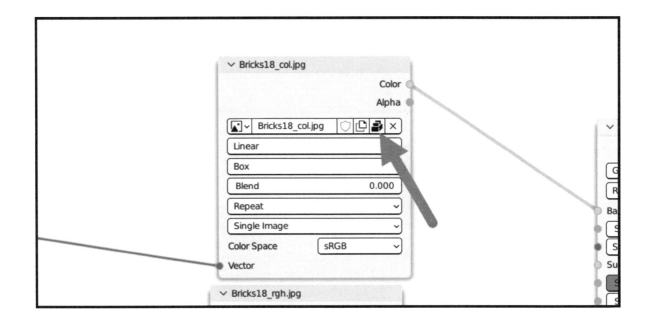

Figure 5.26 - *Unpack item*

Press this icon to extract one image file to the project folder.

Tip: When Blender can't find a texture file, it will show a pink color at your texture file's location. The visual code represents an error where a file is missing. You will have to replace the texture to fix that pink color, which could appear in materials or any other location where you can insert texture files.

5.8 Using multiple materials

What if you want to apply multiple materials for a single object? When you have an object that must receive multiple materials, it is time to use material indexes at the top of your Material tab.

To show how you can use multiple materials with the same object, we can use a simple model like the one shown in Figure 5.27.

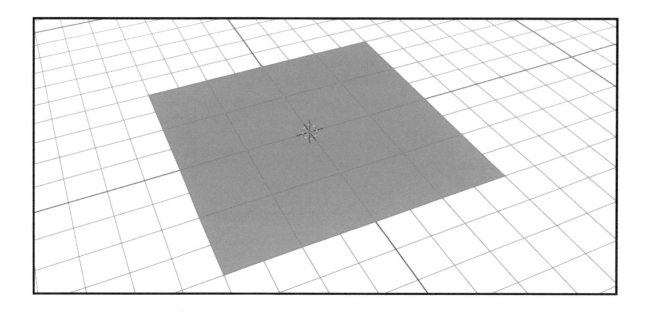

Figure 5.27 - Model with multiple faces

You can make an object like this one with a plane. In Edit Mode, select all vertices and with a right-click open the Context menu. Choose the Subdivide option a few times to create multiple divisions.

You will see additional options at the Material tab when you select any object and go to Edit Mode. Right bellow your indexes selector, you will see buttons for Assign, Select, and Deselect (Figure 5.28).

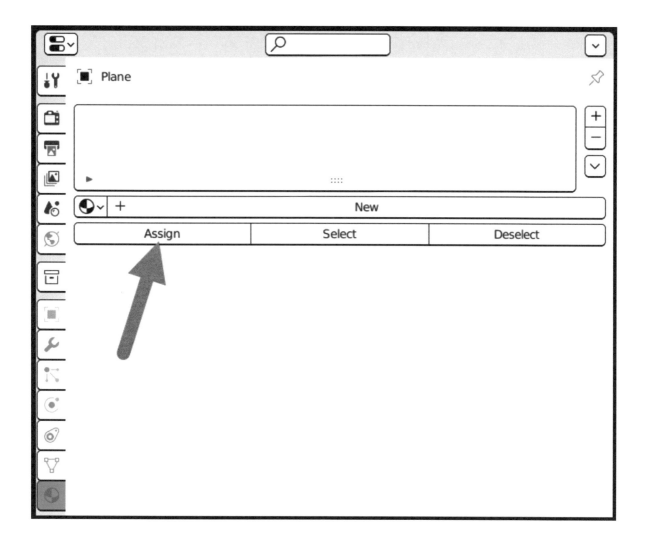

Figure 5.28 - *Material tab in Edit Mode*

For instance, if you can create a new material and assign "Red" as name. Pick the Diffuse BSDF as a shader and make it display a red color. By default, a single material applies to the entire object, and you don't have to do anything else if you only need that one material (Figure 5.29).

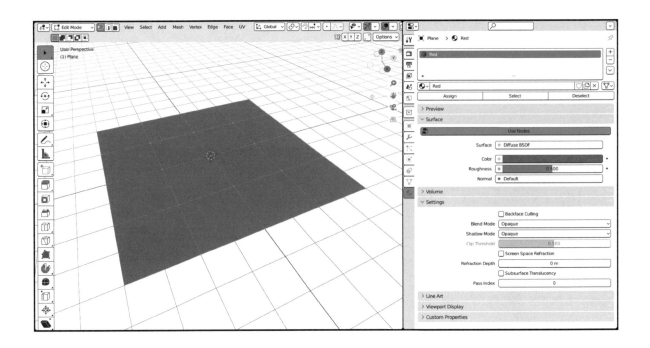

Figure 5.29 - *Red material*

However, we can create another material using the second material index for this selected object. Each object has independent material indexes.

Add another index for that object using the "+" button on the right. Select an existing material or create a new one from scratch. In our case, we can create a simple material called "Green" with a Diffuse BSDF shader and set a green color.

Select half of your object faces, and with the index containing the "Green" material selected, press the Assign button (Figure 5.30).

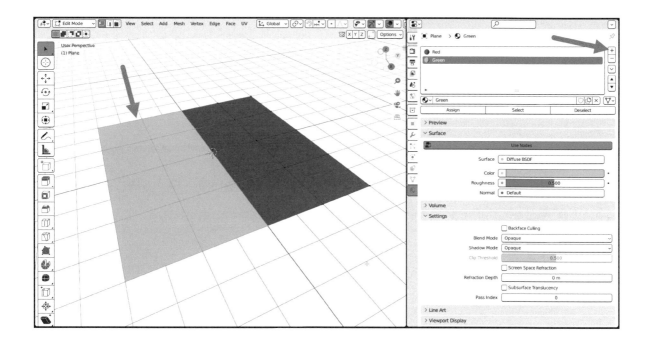

Figure 5.30 - Green material

By the end of the process, you have an object using two materials. If you need more materials for the object, keep adding new indexes and selecting other parts of the model. Mark the elements you want to use and press the Assign button.

What is next?

After adding materials to objects, we are ready for the next step in any project related to 3D visualization, which is rendering and illumination. In Blender, you find two renderers available to generate either still images or animations.

Using Eevee, you will be able to create quick real-time renders from any projects at the cost of realism. Or use Cycles to get photo-real images that might take hours or days to render.

The next chapter teaches you about the render selection and illumination process of scenes using Eevee and Cycles. They share some settings for materials, but lights must receive a few unique adjustments for each renderer.

Chapter 6 - Rendering and illumination

The rendering and illumination of a scene are for many artists, one of the most challenging aspects of a project developed in Blender. To make things even more complicated, you must decide between two render engines. Nowadays, Blender offers Eevee and Cycles.

In the following chapter, you will learn to choose between Cycles or Eevee and prepare lights for a render. To help decide which one to choose, we will show the full process required to set up a scene using both engines.

Besides rendering, you will also learn more about shading and camera setup.

Here is a list of what you will learn:

– Differences between Eevee and Cycles

– How to choose Eevee or Cycles for rendering

– Use shading modes and lights for render

– Adjust the focal length from cameras

– Saving renders as images

– Using environment maps

6.1 Rendering and shading modes

Once you have a 3D model with materials and textures, the next step is to get a render. To render a Blender project, you must decide which is the engine you will want to use. The two options available in Blender are:

– Eevee (*default*)

– Cycles

They are both great renderers that can be useful in specific types of projects. You use Cycles for projects that demand light accuracy and cutting-edge realism. All this quality from Cycles has a high cost in terms of computational power.

As a result, we get longer render times with Cycles, ranging from a couple of minutes, hours, or days for single render. The time required to render a scene depends on several factors like your scene's complexity and the hardware used to render.

Eevee is the new default renderer, which debuted with Blender 2.8 and can work with real-time visualization. Eevee's technology is closer to what we find in modern 3D games, where you will see a less realistic solution for lights and materials but with incredible speed.

You can choose between Eevee and Cycles at the Render tab in your Properties Editor (Figure 6.1).

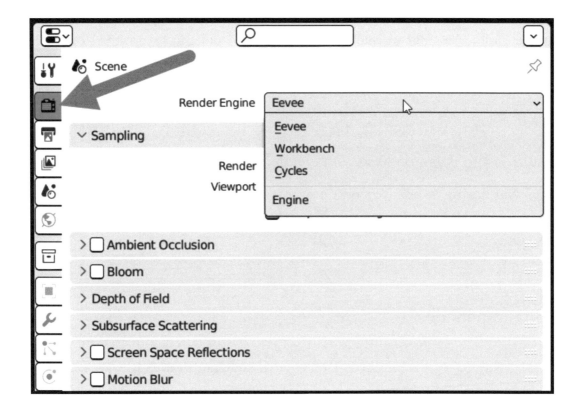

Figure 6.1 - *Render engine selector*

By default, you will always start with Eevee as the main render engine, but you can change to Cycles.

Should you choose Eevee or Cycles for rendering? That depends on your main objective for a project. Here is a quick summary between them:

– **Cycles**: Easier to set up and get realistic results, but might require several minutes or hours to get a finished image.

– **Eevee**: Deliver results in real-time but will not get the same level of realism from Cycles, and requires some pre-processing work to display good looking images.

For materials and lights preview, you can quickly go with Eevee and swap later to Cycles if you decide to use that renderer. Most of the materials work in either renderer without the need to change a lot of settings. That is also valid for PBR materials.

6.1.1 Shading modes

The easiest way to start a render is to use your shading modes in the 3D Viewport. If you look to the right of your header, you see the shading modes (Figure 6.2).

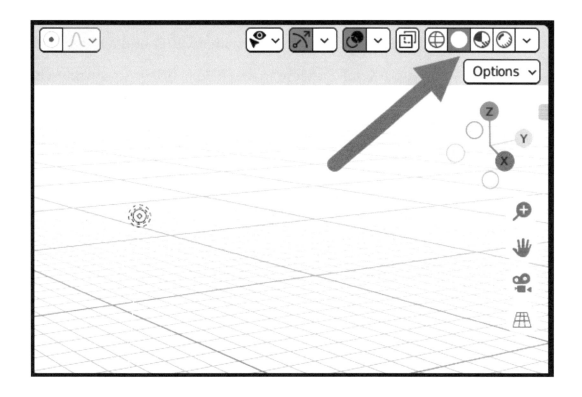

Figure 6.2 - *Shading modes*

With the last button on the right, you get a rendered view from your scene. By using Eevee, you won't notice any slowdowns or performance issues. However, changing the renderer to Cycles might slow down your computer and give you a great impression on the differences between Cycles and Eevee. The reason for a slowdown with Cycles is because it will keep processing the render continuously.

That might get your CPU (*processor*) or GPU (*graphics-card*) usage to 100% load and compromise your computer's performance.

Suppose you want to have a view if your scene with textures and a rough preview of lights, you can use the Material Preview mode. The shortcut to quickly change shading modes is the Z key.

Regarding Viewport shading, you can still choose different lighting modes for the preview and enable Scene Lights and other options. Use the small arrow on your shading modes' right to change the preview display (Figure 6.3).

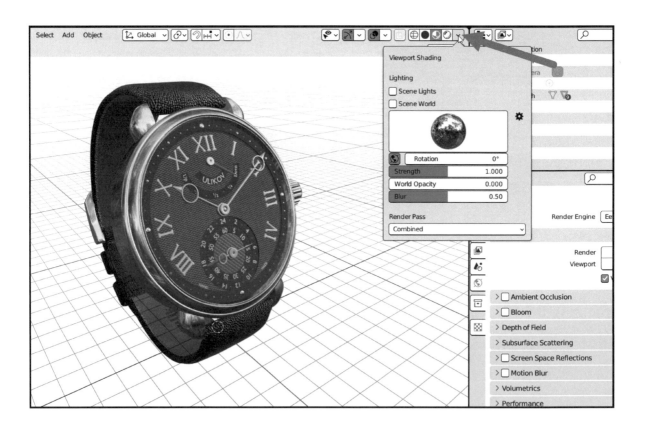

Figure 6.3 - Material Preview options

With Solid shading mode, you have additional options to control transparency and also use colors from the model for material preview and also an option with random colors (Figure 6.4).

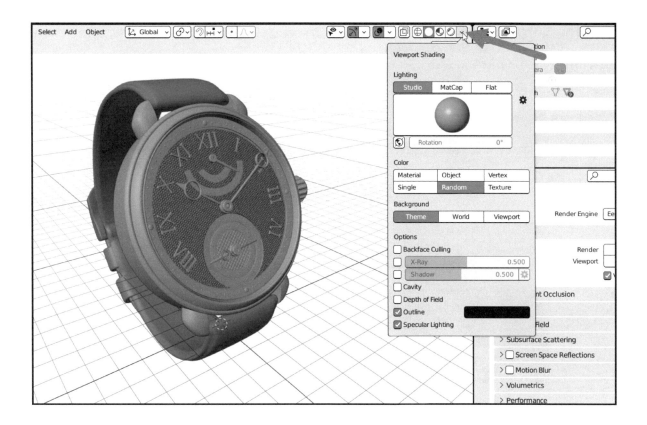

Figure 6.4 - *Solid mode options*

The Rendered shading mode gives a preview for your output render. To save an image from your 3D Viewport during a preview, you can use the **View → Viewport Render Image** menu. That will render any view from the 3D Viewport, and it includes all shading modes.

6.2 Working with cameras

Before we start rendering images from a Blender scene, it is imperative to learn how to manage and adjust cameras. The reason for this is because Blender only renders what the active camera is seeing. That is why you might adjust the view, and when pressing F12 for render, a different angle appears in the render.

You can have several cameras in a scene, but only one of them will be active. The active camera will always show a filled triangle above their icon on the Viewport (Figure 6.5).

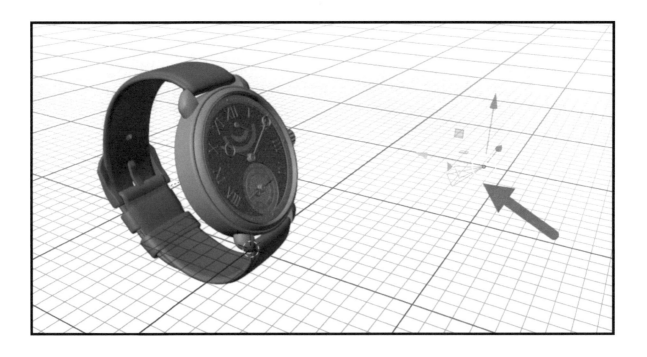

Figure 6.5 - Active camera

You can view what the active camera is currently framing using the Numpad 0 key. It will make you jump to the Camera view (Figure 6.6).

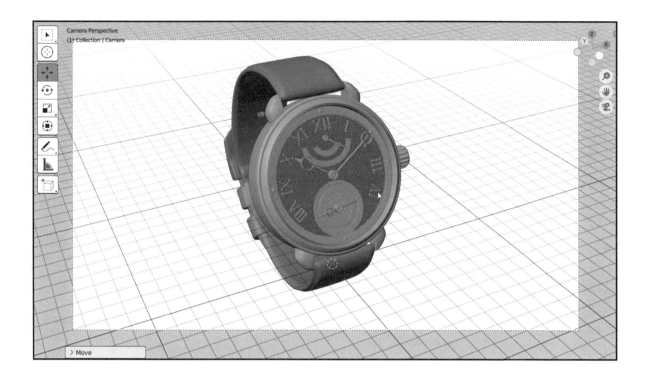

Figure 6.6 - *Camera view*

To make another camera active, select the camera object and press CTRL+Numpad 0. That makes any selected camera active. From the camera view, you can select the camera border and make adjustments to the framing:

– Press the G and R keys to move and rotate the camera

– Press the G key and Z key twice to make a dolly movement

When pressing G and the Z key twice, you will start a dolly movement, where it is possible to move the mouse cursor up and down to move forward and backward. The camera's local Z-axis always points towards the same direction it is currently viewing, which allows us to use those shortcuts.

By pressing an axis key twice, you will use the local coordinates for a transformation instead of global values.

Another way to control your framing for the camera is with the focal distance settings. With the camera object selected, go to the Object Data Properties tab for viewing all camera options (Figure 6.7).

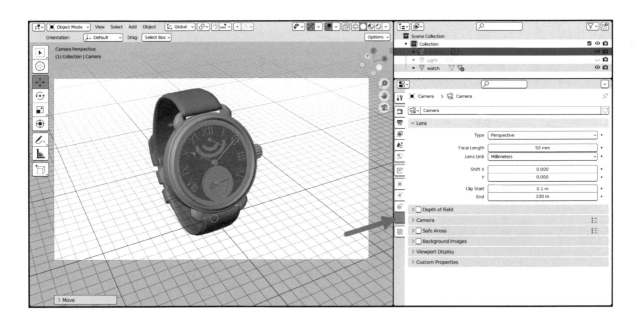

Figure 6.7 - *Camera settings*

At the camera settings, you will find the Focal length at the top. With the Focal length, we can change our camera's viewing angle from the scene (Figure 6.8).

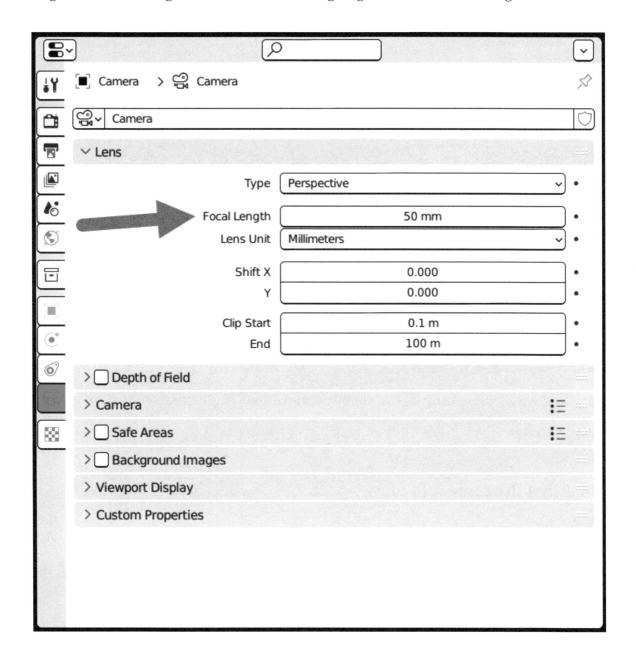

Figure 6.8 - Focal length

Using the millimeters unit, you can get a broad view from the scene with focal distances of 16-20 mm (Figure 6.9). That is how we make a camera to have a wide or narrow view of the scene.

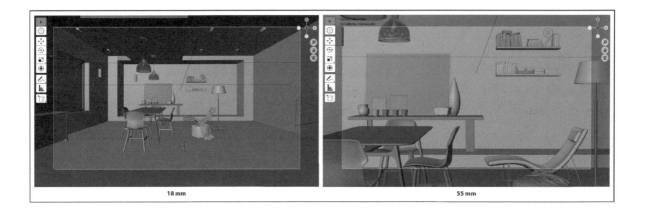

Figure 6.9 - *Focal length difference - Left: 18mm - Right: 55mm*

You have to keep in mind that using lower values for the focal distance might give you a wider view from the scene but will probably add some distortion to your render's borders.

6.2.1 Align the camera to view

Using transformation keys after selecting the camera might help you with an overall framing but will hardly help place the camera for render. The best way to align the camera for rendering is by using 3D Navigation shortcuts.

With the middle mouse button, you can orbit the scene and find a good viewing angle for a render. Once you get the best viewing angle, use a shortcut to align your active camera to that view. Press the CTRL+ALT+Numpad 0 keys.

By pressing those keys simultaneously, you align your active camera with the same viewing angle you have from the scene. It might not still be perfect, but you can make the final adjustments to get a perfect framing using transformation keys.

The option is also available from the **View** → **Align View** → **Align Active Camera to View** menu.

6.3 Rendering scenes

Now that you know how to align cameras in your scene and control viewing angles, it is time to start rendering scenes. To render in Blender, you can either press the F12 key or choose the **Render** → **Render Image** menu.

Once you start a render, you will see the image appearing in the output window. By using Eevee, results will appear in a couple of seconds. In the case of Cycles, it might take a few minutes to finish depending on several factors (Figure 6.10).

Figure 6.10 - *Render results*

The output window always shows what your active camera is currently viewing. If you want to cancel the render at any time, press the ESC key. It may take a while to stop your rendering, especially in Cycles, but it will eventually stop.

6.4 Saving a render

How to save your renders from the Output window in Blender? After having your render results showing in the Output window, use the **Image** menu to save it as an image file. Look for the "Save as…" to save a render (Figure 6.11).

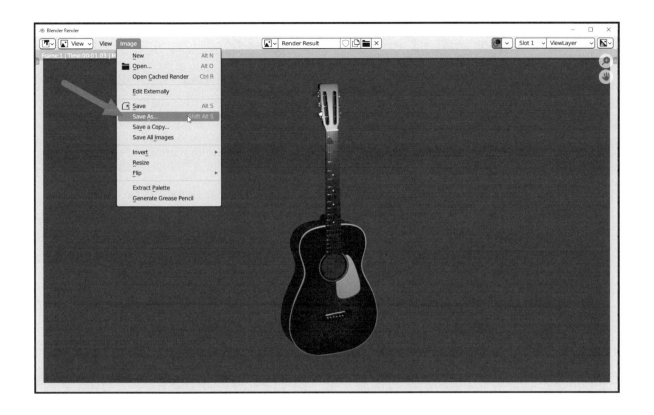

Figure 6.11 - Image menu

A new window appears where it is possible to choose a location to save your render and also an image format. Here are the available options:

– PNG

– JPG

– TGA

– TIFF

– EXR

To always keep your render results with the highest possible quality, always save your projects as PNG files first. If you need a smaller version, you can convert the PNG to a JPG file later. Depending on your project, you might want to use EXR for post-processing. But, in most cases, a PNG is the best choice.

The reason to keep your renders as PNG files is because it uses a type of compression for images called *lossless*. With this method, you get larger file sizes but with no data loss from your renders. It is a compression similar to what ZIP containers do with text files.

On the other hand, a JPG file uses a compression method called *lossy*, which excludes some information to reduce file size. Every time you save a JPG file, the algorithm will exclude data from your image to reduce file size.

For that reason, try to save all renders as PNG files first and then convert them to JPG later if you need a smaller file.

6.4.1 Image settings for rendering

An important setting for any render in Blender is the resolution of your images, which is also a factor that can determine how long it will take for a render to finish. For instance, rendering an image with 300 x 200 pixels finishes a lot faster than a 4K image with 4096 x 2160 pixels.

Resolution settings are available in the Output Properties tab at the Properties Editor (Figure 6.12).

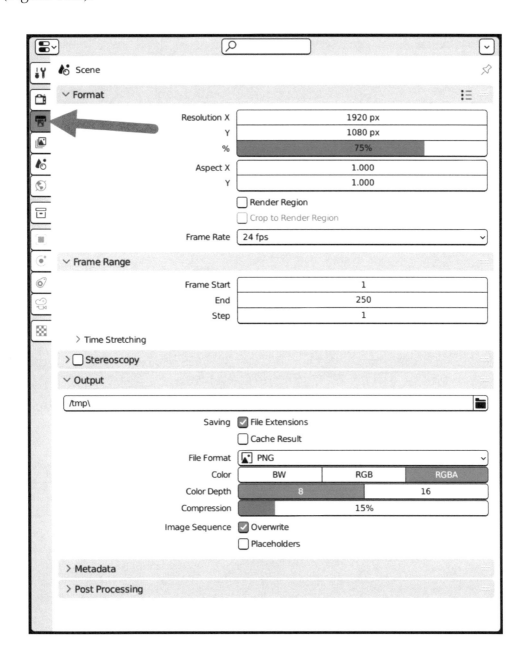

Figure 6.12 - Output settings

In the settings, you can manually type the size you wish to use for a render or get an industry-standard resolution from several presets (Figure 6.13).

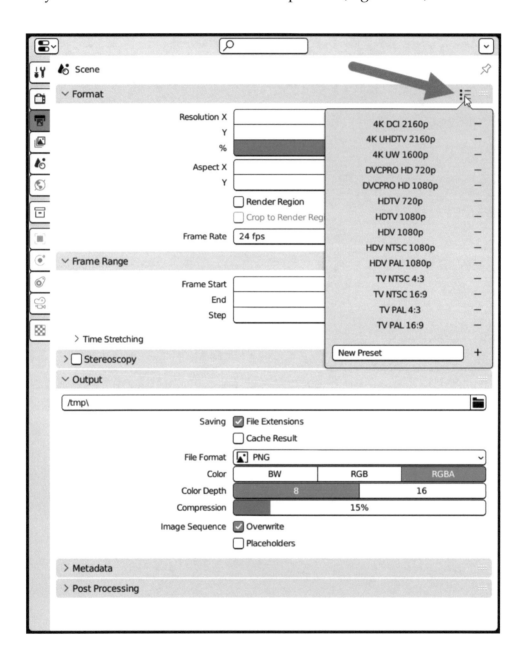

Figure 6.13 - *Resolution settings*

You can also choose your image format in the Output Properties tab and color settings. One of the benefits of using a PNG file besides the quality is using the RGBA color format. By using RGBA, you can have transparent pixels in your images (Figure 6.14).

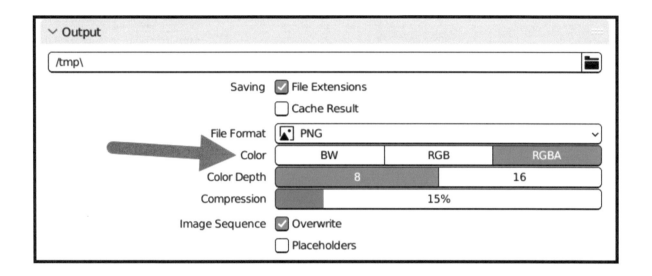

Figure 6.14 - *Color settings*

That is useful to make renders with a transparent background. To render images with no background, go to the Film settings and enable an option called "Transparent" to make your renders appear with a transparent background. Having transparent pixels is useful to compose renders with other images. The option works for Cycles or Eevee (Figure 6.15).

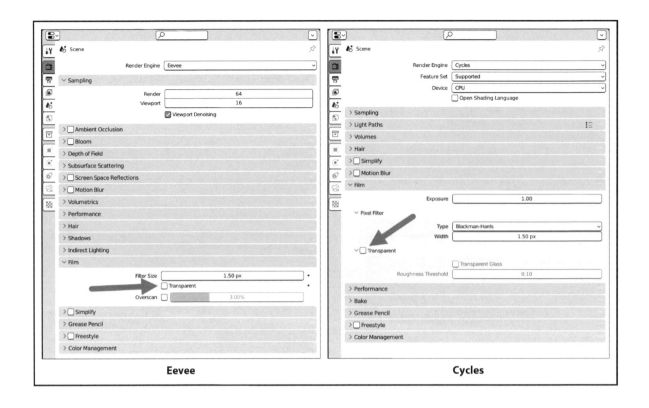

Figure 6.15 - Transparent option

The JPG format used by Blender doesn't support transparent backgrounds, which will add a solid color instead of transparent pixels as a background in case you save the render results in JPG format.

6.5 Environmental lights

One of the first steps many artists take when starting to work on lights for a scene in Blender is to add an environmental light. That is a light coming from a scene's background, which could add a significant amount of energy to the entire 3D space.

For that purpose, we can either use a plain color as the background or add a special type of textures like an HDR image. An HDR texture is useful for your environmental lights because:

– They store information about lights for the moment the map got created.

– Since your image stays in the background, it will reflect on glossy surfaces across the scene.

– It may work as the background for your scene.

For instance, if you get an HDR image with bright sky daylight and add it to your scene's background, it will generate the same type of lights for the render (Figure 6.16).

Figure 6.16 - Daylight HDR

How to use an HDR in your background? Add an HDR in the World Properties tab at the Properties Editor. There you will find a field called Surface options. Press the "Use Nodes" button and go to the Color field. Click at the small button with a yellow circle on the left, and pick "Environment Texture" (Figure 6.17).

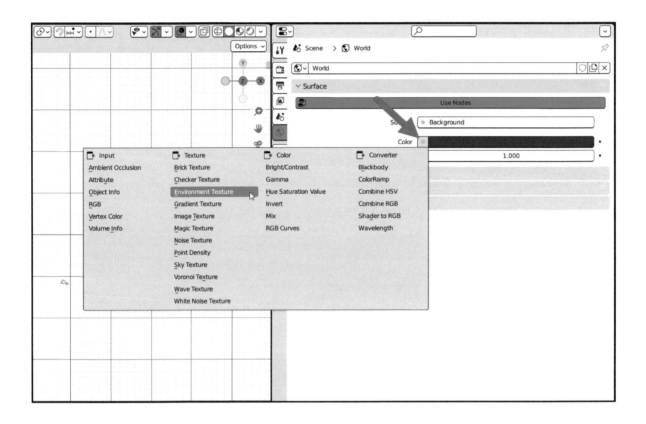

Figure 6.17 - Environment Texture

Once you add the Environment Texture to the Color, a small set of options appears with a button to open a file. Click at the "Open" button and get an HDR map from your computer or local network. It appears as your scene's background if you use the rendered shading mode (Figure 6.18).

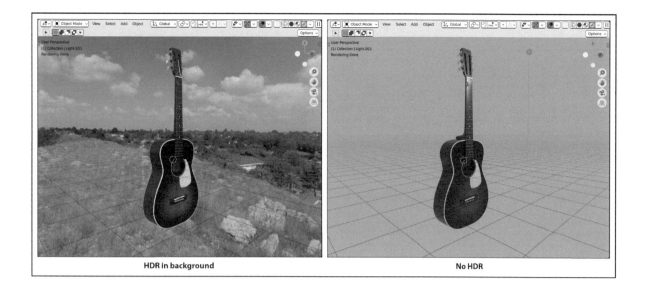

Figure 6.18 - *HDR in the background*

If you don't like how your HDR map appears in the background, it is possible to change all mapping aspects of your map, like rotation. Open the Shader Editor and change the View option to World (Figure 6.19).

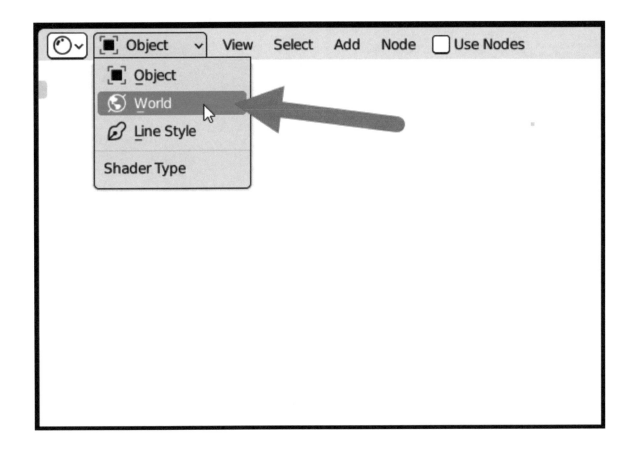

Figure 6.19 - *Shader Editor view*

It displays Nodes related to the World Properties tab, and the HDR map will be there for editing. Add the same Texture Coordinates and Mapping Nodes we used back in chapter 5 (Figure 6.20).

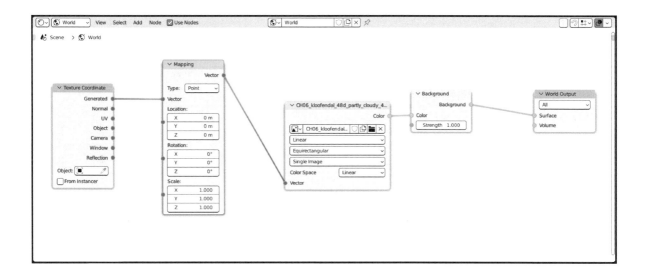

Figure 6.20 - *Nodes for rotation*

Connect the Texture Coordinates and the Mapping to the Image Texture Node, and you will be able to control HDR rotation with the Rotation settings from the Mapping Node.

A few points regarding HDR maps for both Cycles and Eevee:

– In Cycles, you will get lights and shadows from HDR maps.

– Eevee can't cast shadows from HDR maps, which makes them less useful for real-time render.

– An HDR map might create different types of lighting. That depends on the location and timing used as a source for each HDR. Usually, you can get an idea about the lighting in the library's preview, where you download the HDR map.

You can get dozens of free HDR maps for your projects from *hdrhaven.com* as public domain files. They offer multiple types of lights and locations with maps with resolutions going up to 8K *(8192 pixels)*.

Tip: *You can download public domain HDR maps from hdrihaven.com for any project in Blender.*

6.6 Illumination and types of lights

Environment lights will be a great help as a starting point for any project, but you will also need additional light sources. For instance, if you use Eevee for rendering, a light source will be the best choice to replace an HDR map since it can't cast shadows in real-time.

In Blender, you can create several types of lights with the SHIFT+A key (Figure 6.21).

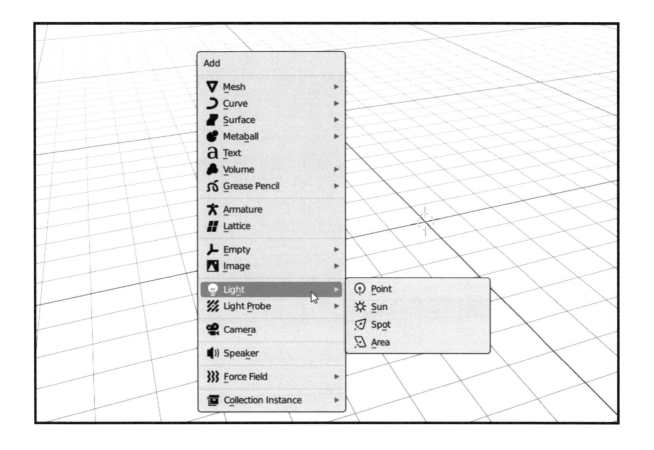

Figure 6.21 - *Lights options*

The list has options for lights includes:

– **Point**: Emit light from a single point in space in all directions.

– **Sun**: Simulate a distant light source that behaves like the Sun.

– **Spot**: A point that cast light in a cone shape.

– **Area**: A squared shape that emits lights from all the available shapes.

Each one of those lights has a purpose in a project. For instance, in a scene that tries to simulate daylight, you will probably use a Sun combined with an HDR map for a Cycles render.

It is possible to add each new lights using the SHIFT+A key or change an existing light source type by selecting it and opening the Object Data tab. There you will see buttons at the top where you can quickly swap between each type of light (Figure 6.22).

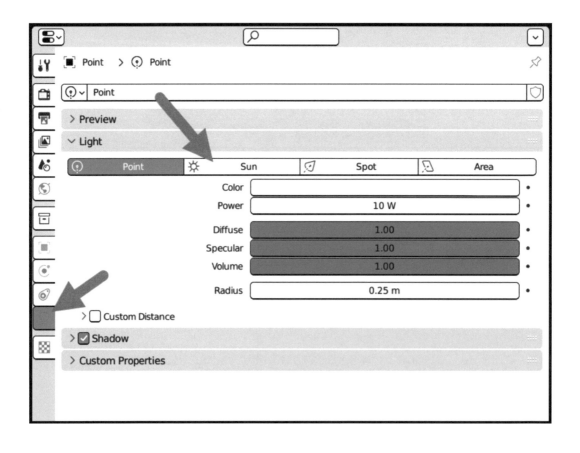

Figure 6.22 - *Light types*

The Object Data tab also displays options regarding lights where you can control:

– Shadows

– Color

– Power

Besides those settings, you will also find contextual options for each light type. For instance, in the Area light options, you will set the size of your light plane. The Spot will show controls for a cone projection.

Options for each light also change based on your renderer selection. In Figure 6.23, you can see a comparison between settings for an Area light with Eevee and Cycles. Notice how they offer unique options based on each renderer.

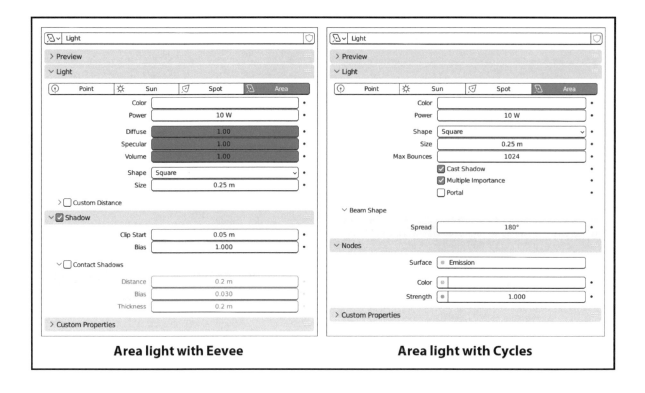

Figure 6.23 - *Comparing light settings*

You will see the most significant difference in the shadow settings with more options to control shadows when you select Eevee as a renderer.

6.7 Quick setup for rendering

Since each renderer requires specific settings to achieve good lighting results, we will use a simple scene shown in Figure 6.24 to apply a quick setup using both Eevee and Cycles. In the process, we can tweak settings for lights and shadows.

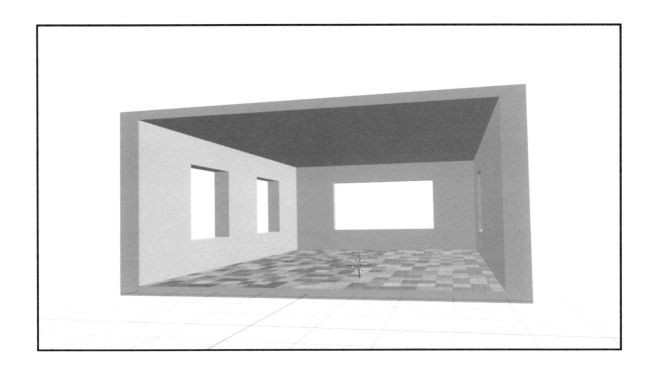

Figure 6.24 - *Scene for quick setup*

From that scene, you will learn how to prepare a project for rendering with both engines.

Unfortunately, it is hard to replicate the same settings for all scenes in a 3D project. That happens because each scene has unique needs and aspects, which might demand adjustments from the author.

However, you can use the following quick setup as a starting point for future projects and adapt each case's settings.

6.7.1 Quick setup for render with Eevee

To render a scene in Eevee, we have to consider a few details regarding renderer. You need special attention to:

– **Indirect Lights**: Eevee can't generate indirect lights from light sources alone. We have to use probes to calculate indirect bounces.

– **Reflections**: Another feature that you will have to emulate with probes are reflections from glossy surfaces.

– **Environment lights**: With Eevee, you won't get shadows from HDR maps used as the background (*Environment texture*). One of the best choices to replace HDR maps is an Area Light.

– **Light bleed**: A problem that you may encounter in projects rendered with Eevee is light bleed. That might appear due to several factors like 3D models with walls that don't have any thickness or shadows settings.

As a first step for the scene, you should add an Area Light that will work as an environment light. Since Eevee doesn't support shadow casting from HDR maps, an Area Light is a great option to use in the background.

Using the rotation and move shortcuts, place the light source in the scene's background, far away from the model. Use the light settings to increase the size of that Area Light until it became larger than the model.

Enable Shadows and also Contact Shadows (Figure 6.25).

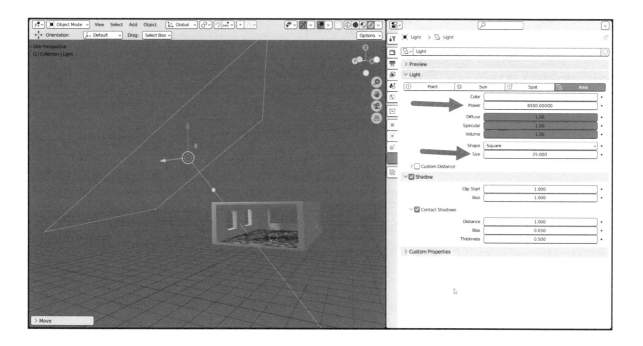

Figure 6.25 - *Area as the environmental light*

Besides an Area Light in the background, you can also add one Area Light to each of the windows to increase the scene's illumination. Use the size settings from the lights to adjust them to each Area Light (Figure 6.26). Scale them until they fit in each window.

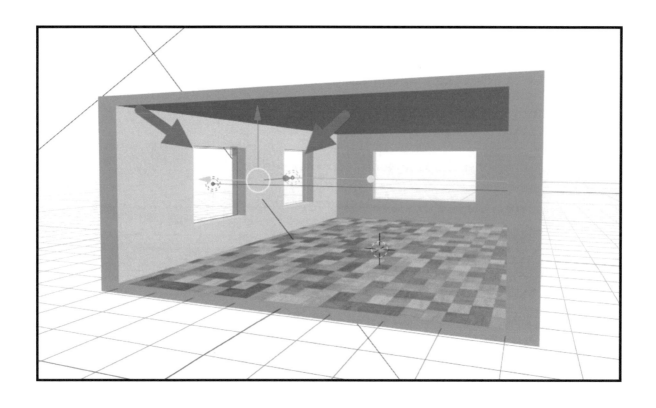

Figure 6.26 - *Area lights in windows*

Since Eevee can't handle indirect lights for rendering, we have to use a helper object for those calculations. The helper objects for Eevee have the name of Probes.

For indirect lights, you use a probe called Irradiance Volume. Press the SHIFT+A keys, and from the Light Probes group, add an Irradiance Volume. Select the Irradiance Volume and use the S key scale until it covers the entire scene (Figure 6.27).

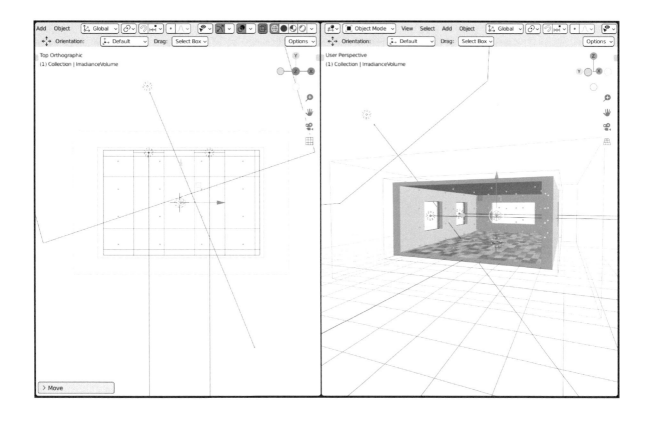

Figure 6.27 - *Irradiance Volume in the scene*

The Irradiance Volume has a box-like shape, and it identifies an area where Eevee will later process indirect light bounces. Only what is inside the Probe volume receives indirect light bounces. You can add as many of those Probes as you need.

The next probe we will need is a Reflection Cubemap that captures reflections and cast them in glossy surfaces. Press SHIFT+A again and from the Light Probes group, add a Reflection Cubemap. Using the G key, raise the probe from the ground level and place it in your scene's middle.

Unlike an Irradiance Volume with a box-like shape, a Reflection Cubemap has a default shape of a sphere. Use a scale transformation to increase your probe's size until it becomes bigger than your scene (Figure 6.28).

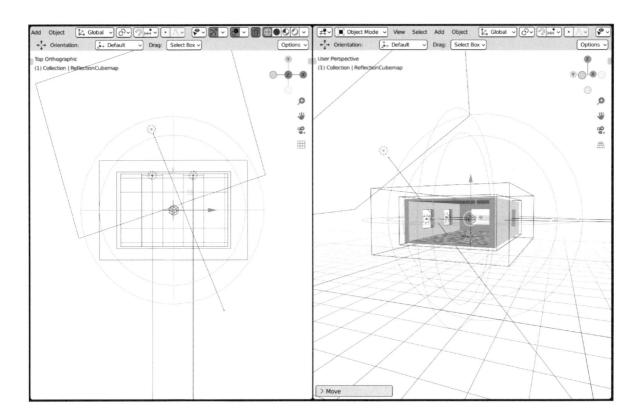

Figure 6.28 - Reflection Cubemap

It is time to use the settings from the Render tab in the Properties Editor. Locate the Indirect Lighting settings and press Bake Indirect Lighting. It starts to calculate indirect lights and reflections for all Probes (Figure 6.29).

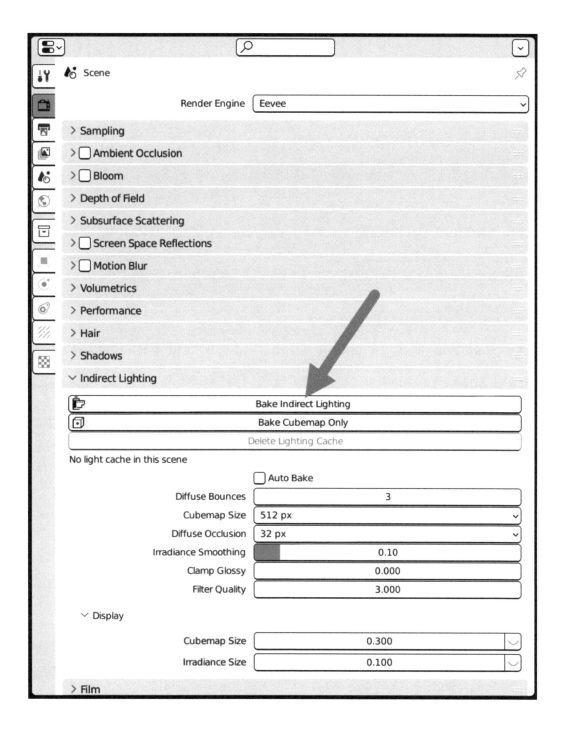

Figure 6.29 - *Indirect lights baking*

You will see a progress bar at the bottom of your interface. It can take a couple of seconds or minutes to process all Probes, which depends on your scene's complexity.

We can make additional enhancements to the scene by:

– **Enable Ambient Occlusion**: That will generate contact shadows.

– **Enable Screen Space Reflections**: To create reflections based on a mirror image of your scene.

– **In the Shadows settings, enable High Bitdepth and Soft Shadows**: To increase all shadows' quality.

– **In the Shadow settings, change the Cube Size and Cascade Size for 1024px and 2048px, respectively**: That will create better borders for all shadows.

Before you render the scene, use the rendered shading mode from Eevee to adjust lights even further using Color Management options (Figure 6.30).

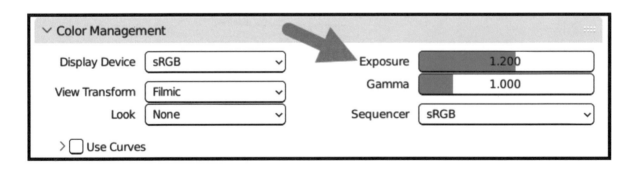

Figure 6.30 - *Color Management*

With the exposure settings, you can increase the brightness of the scene (Figure 6.31). It is also possible to change settings from Color Management after finishing a render.

Exposure = 1.2

Exposure = 2.4

Figure 6.31 - *Exposure settings*

If you press the F12 key after using all those settings, you will get the Eevee's rendered image at the Output Window.

The workflow is a basic guide on how to prepare any scene to render in real-time. It may not be the most accurate visualization of a scene regarding realism, but it is fast. It might not work for all types of projects, but you can use it as a starting point.

Tip: Use the settings from the Output tab to choose the resolution for your render images.

6.7.2 Quick setup for render with Cycles

Unlike Eevee, you can use a more direct approach with Cycles, and it doesn't require any type of probe to calculate indirect lights. However, you might have to wait a little longer for the render to finish.

The first thing you must do is to set the current render as Cycles.

With Cycles, we can use an HDR map for environmental light to give an initial boost in the scene lighting. Go to the World tab and add an HDR map to the background (Figure 6.32).

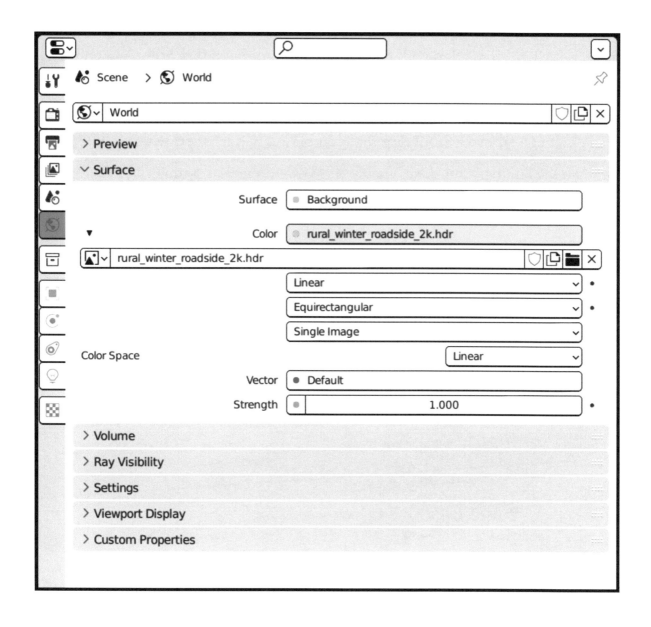

Figure 6.32 - HDR in the background

Adjust your HDR map's power level in the World tab, and we can move on to the next step.

Tip: You can download dozens of free HDR maps from hdrihaven.com at no cost.

271

For a daylight simulation with Cycles, use two types of lights; Sun Light and Area Lights.

The first one will be a Sun Light that you placed in a location where you want to simulate the Sun position. Also, enable shadows in the Sun settings and change the Angle value to a number close to zero like "0.05" to get hard edge shadows (Figure 6.33).

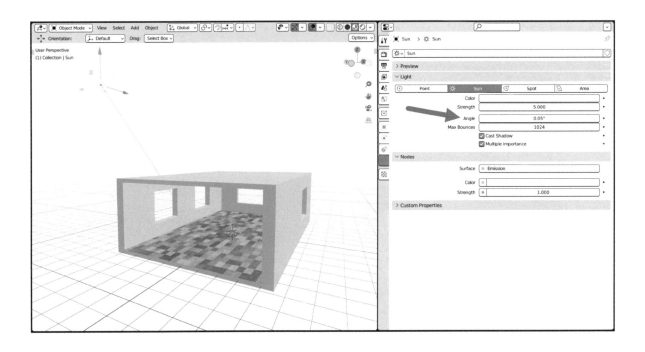

Figure 6.33 - Sun settings

You can use the R key to rotate the Sun and find a location where the light beams will more efficiently enter your scene.

In some cases, using a Sun Light alone won't add the necessary energy to the scene. For that reason, we need a second source. Using Area lights in each window will also help with that type of project.

Disable shadow casting for those lights and also scale each Area Light until they fit the same size of each window (Figure 6.34).

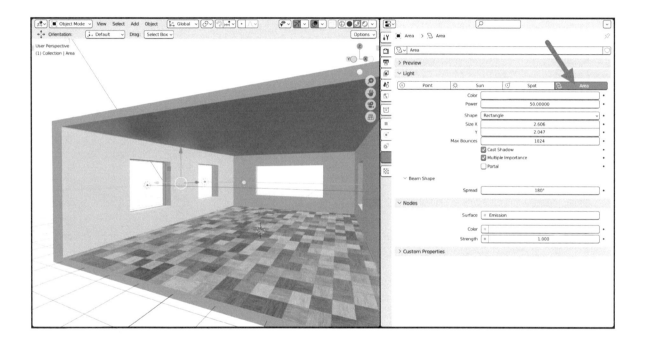

Figure 6.34 - *Area light settings*

As part of the process of getting lights with the best possible settings, you will have to play with the Strength settings for all sources to find the appropriate balance. The same values won't work for all types of projects.

If you use the Rendered Shading mode for Cycles at this point, you will have a great idea of Eevee's differences. The render progress displays a slow process, starting with a grainy image that stops at 1024 interactions (Figure 6.35).

Figure 6.35 - Render preview with Cycles

Those interactions in Cycles have a limit that you can adjust at the Render tab.

Tip: You can interrupt the render for your preview using the pause button next to the shading modes selector.

In the Sampling field, you find the limit for interactions for both the Render and Previews. The default value for your 3D Viewport (*Previews*) starts with a minimum of 0 and a maximum of 1024 (Figure 6.36).

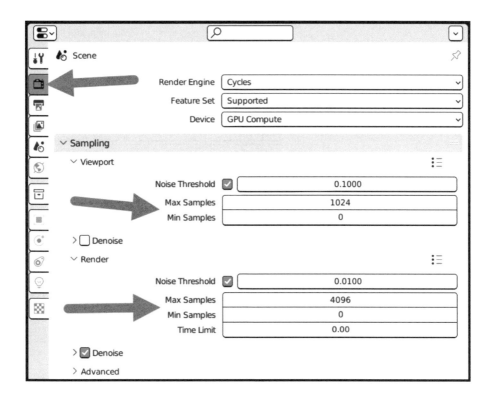

Figure 6.36 - *Render settings*

One of the biggest challenges to render a scene in Cycles is finding an optimal sample limit that will give you a noiseless image. Usually, a value between 500 and 1000 gives you good results, but it depends on several factors. The difference in render times from 500 to 1000 samples could be a few minutes or hours.

To help you using fewer samples for a faster render, we can enable the Denoiser tool in Cycles. Go to the Sampling options and enable the Denoiser tool. Below your Sampling settings, you can enable the Denoiser for either the render or Viewport. The Viewport option removes noise from a render preview (Figure 6.37).

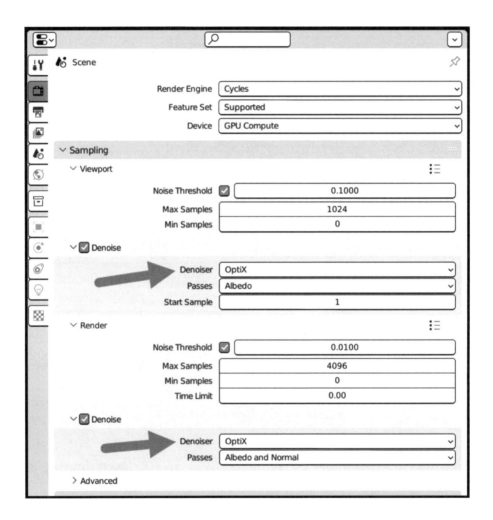

Figure 6.37 - Denoiser tool

The Denoiser applies a "blur" filter for a render that will remove a considerable amount of noise from renders. It is not a perfect solution but helps a lot in reducing render times.

You can also choose from three different types of methods for Denoising:

– **NLM:** The standard method to remove noise from renders.

– **OpenImageDenoise:** Here, we have a powerful denier filter that uses machine learning to removes noise from an image.

– **OptiX:** If you have an RTX graphics-card from NVIDIA, you can use the artificial intelligence-powered OptiX denier. It is also an impressive denier filter that can dramatically speed up renders. You must select OptiX from the Cycles settings to use this method.

That will give you room to use fewer samples and still get a clean image. Even with the Denoiser options, you will have to perform a few tests to find the optimal sample value for your project.

In our case, a sample count with a maximum of 500 with the Denoiser enabled gives good results. After changing the max samples, adjust the camera and start your render. Since we are using Cycles, our render will probably take a few minutes to process.

The total render time for this particular render was 11 seconds, using the GPU to speed up the process.

You can select the GPU for rendering in the Render tab (Figure 6.38).

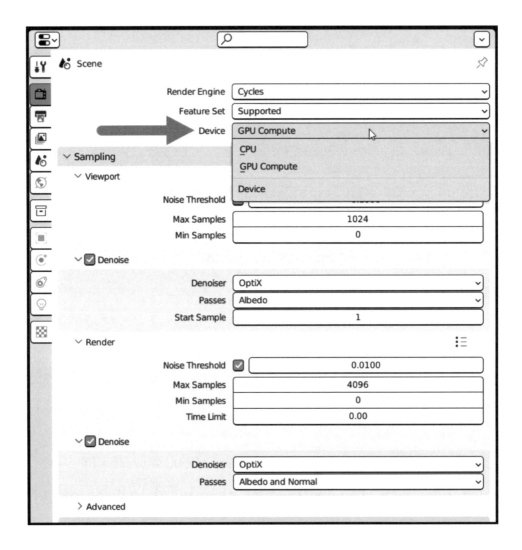

Figure 6.38 - Choosing the GPU

It is possible to select your graphics-card to process a scene from Cycles in the Device field. If you don't see the GPU option, go to the **Edit → Preferences** menu, and open the System tab. There you have a list with the Cycles Render Devices (Figure 6.39).

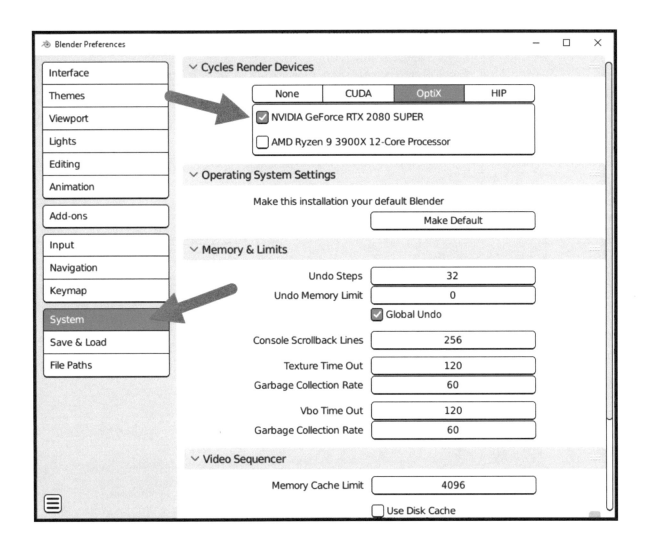

Figure 6.39 - Using GPU to speedup renders

For Radeon cards from AMD, you must select the OpenCL field, and for NVIDIA, you can use either CUDA or OptiX. The CUDA option will already add a huge boost to your renders, and for maximum speed, you can enable OptiX. However, not all features from Cycles are compatible with OptiX.

In any case, you should use the GPU if you have one available on the computer used for render. Just remember that your scene must fit in the VRAM space for processing. Otherwise, you will have to use the CPU only.

After you render the project, it is time to make adjustments to your scene's brightness with the Color Management options (Figure 6.40).

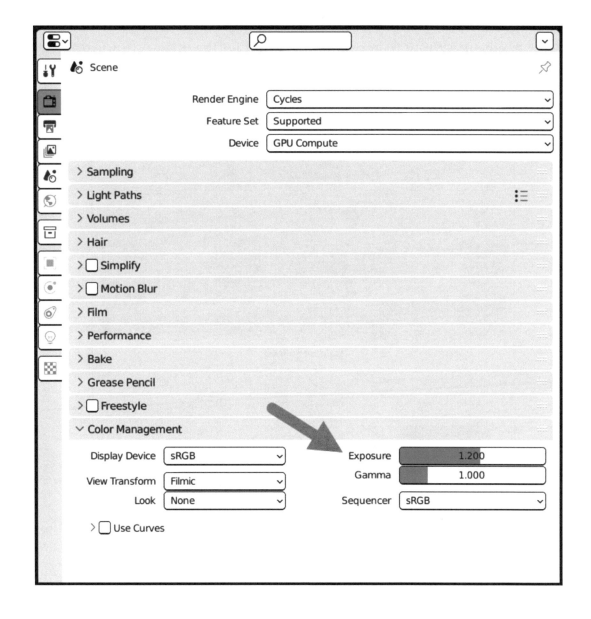

Figure 6.40 - *Color management*

It is possible to change your render looks using options from the Color Management field, even after a render ended. It might give you a lot of flexibility to tweak lights and also color settings.

Use the exposure settings to get a brighter result for the image (Figure 6.41).

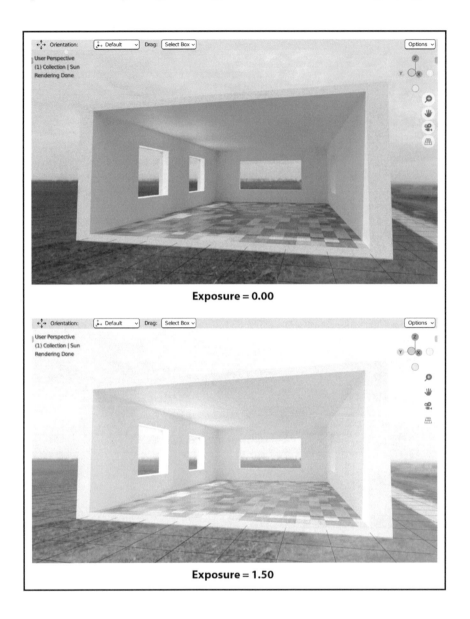

Figure 6.41 - *Exposure results*

Save the render results to disk, and you have a full render in Cycles.

What is next?

Unlike many aspects of projects related to 3D modeling where you repeat steps and tools to build a complex object, working with rendering and lighting is different and requires an approach for each scene.

That is because each project features unique settings for scale, materials, and context. For that reason, you must find the best adjustment for each new scene. With practice, you will learn that most scenes can share settings for environment lights and materials.

But for lights setup, you will have to adjust in each scene—even the sampling values changes.

What will give you confidence with rendering is practice! A great way to develop your skills for lighting is by observing an image like a photo an trying to reproduce the effect and shading with the options in Blender.

As a follow-up to our rendering chapter, you find in chapter 7 instructions on creating videos and sequences of images for animations. Blender is a powerful software to create animations, and you will learn how to add keyframes to develop all kinds of motion.

Chapter 7 - Animation and motion with Blender

Do you know that even when rendering a single image in Blender, you handle animation? One of the primary purposes of Blender is to create animations, and it has lots of features and tools to create motion graphics.

In this chapter, you will learn how to create an animation using one of the animation foundations, which is the keyframe. The keyframes allow us to mark a certain property in time for animation. A key component of animation consists of having objects with multiple keyframes in a Timeline. That allows us to work with something called interpolation.

We will cover how to manage and use those keyframes for interpolation-based animation. Here is a list of what you will learn in this chapter:

  – How animations work in Blender

  – Controlling and managing frames and length for animations

  – Add/Remove and manage keyframes

  – Creating simple animations with keyframes

  – Making linear animations using curves

7.1 How to make an animation with Blender?

The method Blender uses to create animations has a name of interpolation, which works based on a combination of keyframes and transformations along a Timeline. Each keyframe "marks" a property of an object at a certain point in time.

You can think of an animation as a sequence of still images. When using a certain speed to reproduce them, you have the illusion of motion. Each still image in animation has a name of frame.

An interpolation animation uses the different values of a property to create motion. For instance, if an animation has 50 frames where you set a property with a value of 200 at frame 1, and a value of 500 at frame 50.

The interpolation method calculates a proportional progression between frames 2 and 49. If you have enough keyframes in a Timeline, an animation appears when you hit the play button.

A Timeline for animations uses frames to identify the time. Usually, an animation has 24 to 30 frames for one second of animation. For instance, if you get an animation that has 5 seconds with 30 frames per second requires 150 frames.

The rate of frames displayed per second has a name of frame rate, and it appears in lots of places with the acronym FPS. For the rest of the book, we will use FPS to identify frame rates.

By default, you always start with an FPS of 24, which you can change at the Output tab (Figure 7.1).

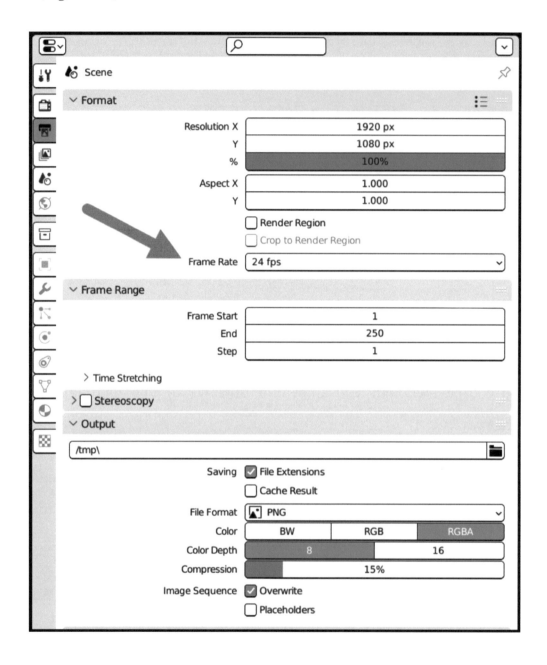

Figure 7.1 - *Frame rate settings*

For video and animation, most artists use either 24 or 30 FPS. Since animations can also consume many resources, Blender limits the total length with a start and end frames. Above the frame rate settings, you can set the start and end frames in your current scene (Figure 7.2).

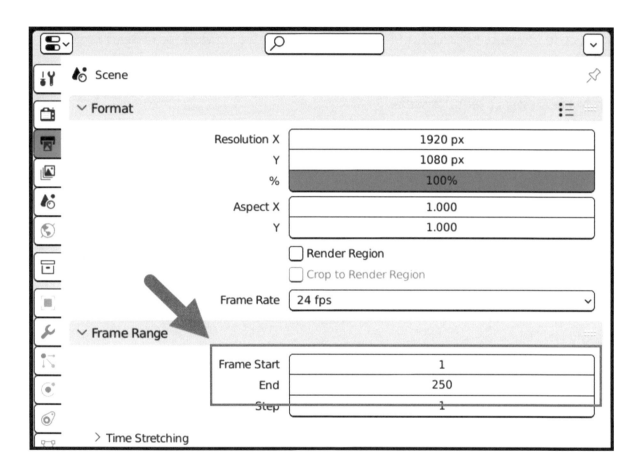

Figure 7.2 - Start and end frames

Those values always start with 1 and 250 for start and end, respectively. If you have to create an animation with 3 seconds using a 30 FPS, which requires 90 frames, you can keep the start to 1 and set the end to 90.

If you don't change the start and end, all animations in Blender will occur be-tween frames 1 and 250. You can still create a 90 frames animation and don't touch the start and end frames.

However, when hitting the play button to preview your motion, it will go from frame 1 to 250 and not stop at 90. That is also true for rendering. Instead of render-ing 90 frames, you will process 250. Always change the start and end frames accord-ing to your project requirements.

7.1.1 Adding keyframes to objects

To add keyframes in Blender, we can use several methods from keyboard shortcuts to the Context menu. No matter the way used to create keyframes, you won't be able to make animations without them. After selecting an object, you can use the I key to add a keyframe. That is the easiest way to add keyframes to anything in Blender.

Once you press the I key, a list with all available keyframe types appears (Figure 7.3).

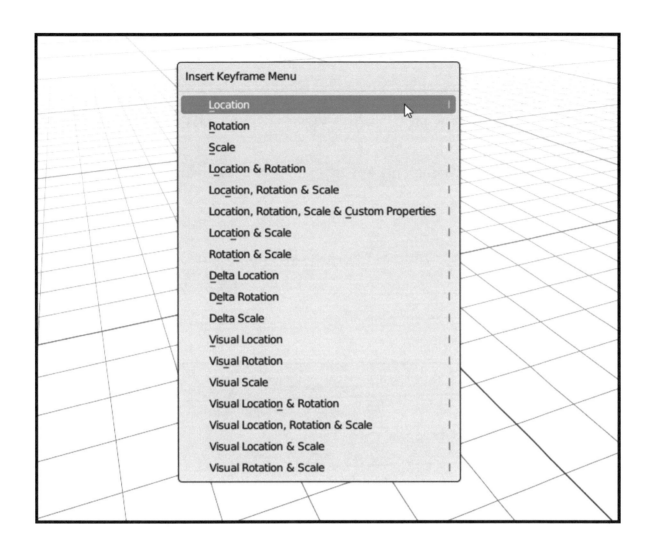

Figure 7.3 - *Keyframe types*

You must choose the keyframe type based on the kind of animation data needed for a project. The keyframe type has a direct relation to the property you are animating.

For instance, if you are trying to animate a rotation, you will create a keyframe using the Rotation keyframe type. In case you want to make a rotation and scale animation at the same time, you can use the RotScale keyframe type.

The keyframe type selection only appears when you are creating keyframes in the 3D Viewport.

Another way to insert keyframes to objects is with a right-click on the 3D Viewport. Using the Context menu, you can choose "Insert keyframe..." to add keyframes (Figure 7.4).

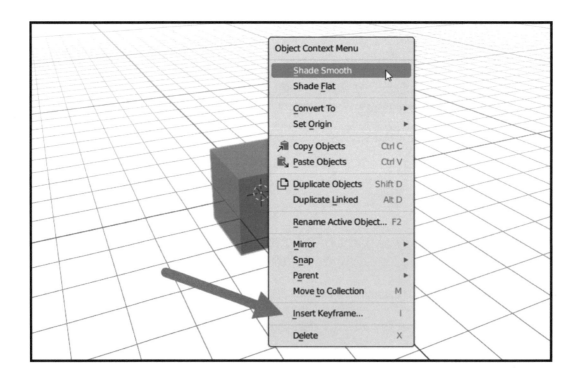

Figure 7.4 - Context menu

By the way, always create keyframes in *Object Mode* for animation!

It is also possible to add keyframes in the 3D Viewport Sidebar, or using the Object tab at the Properties Editor. If you right-click at any property like a location, you will see keyframe options (Figure 7.5).

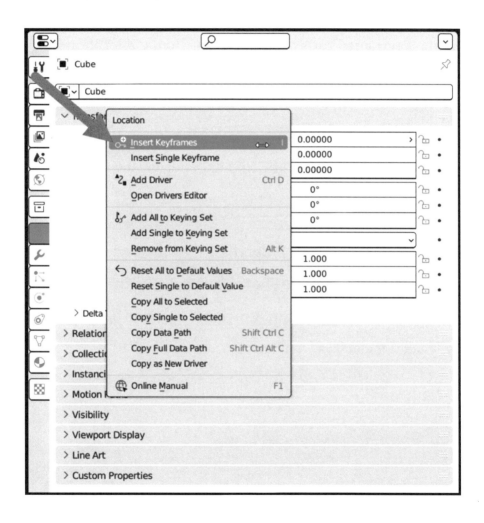

Figure 7.5 - Inserting keyframes in properties

For instance, if you right-click at the X Location field:

– **Insert keyframes**: Creates a keyframe for all three axes in the location property.

– **Insert Single Keyframe**: Adds a keyframe only to the X location property.

By using the right-click at single option properties, you won't have to choose keyframe types. You will have to choose whether adding the keyframe to a single property or all three (X, Y, and Z-axis). That depends on the type of animation you need.

After adding a keyframe to those properties, a yellow background appears at the property editor. That is a visual code showing a keyframe that exists at that property in the current frame. On the right, notice that a diamond-shaped symbol appears instead of the small dot available in all properties (Figure 7.6).

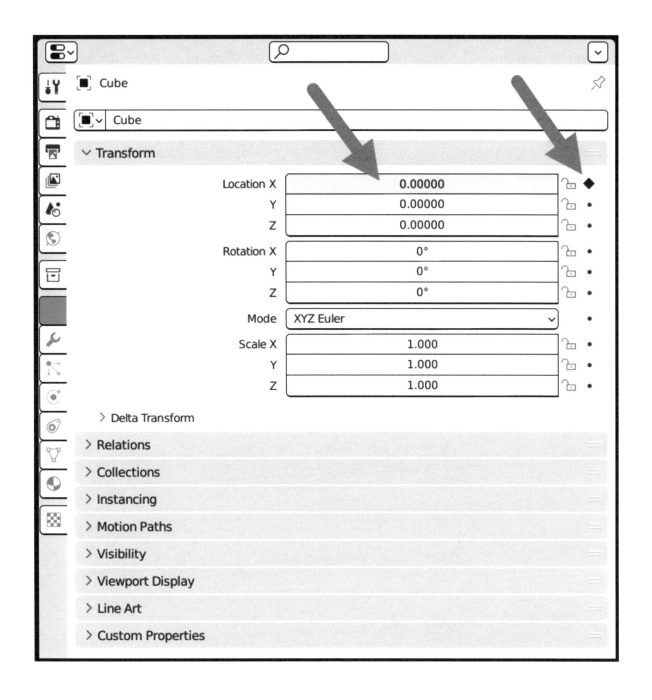

Figure 7.6 - *Keyframe in property*

Another way to add keyframes to any object is by clicking at those dots, which will make the diamond shape icon appear. It identifies an existing keyframe for that property.

Info: The interpolation process uses the keyframes to create animations. It takes the difference in properties between two keyframes to generate all intermediate values automatically.

7.1.2 Removing and updating keyframes

What if you want to remove a keyframe? You can easily remove and manage keyframes with a right-click on a property value that has a keyframe. If you right-click, a menu with several options to manage keyframes appears (Figure 7.7).

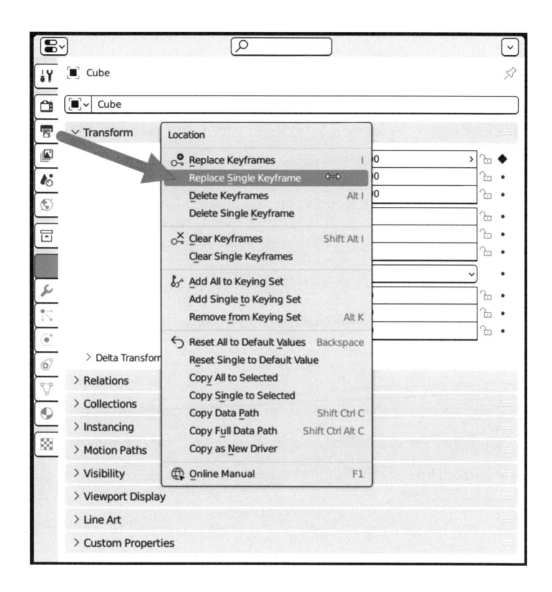

Figure 7.7 - *Managing keyframes*

There is more than one option to manage keyframes:

– **Replace keyframes**: Updates all keyframes' property value and keeps them in the same locations in time.

– **Replace Single Keyframe**: Changes the value of your selected keyframe for that particular moment in time.

– **Delete Keyframes**: Removes all keyframes from the object for that specific property in a single frame.

– **Delete Single Keyframe**: Excludes only the selected keyframe for that frame.

– **Clear Keyframes**: Removes all keyframes in all properties for the entire Timeline.

– **Clear Single keyframes**: Removes all keyframes for the property selected in all Timeline.

Notice that you can use either the Delete or Clear keyframes to remove animation data from an object. The difference between them is that you will remove keyframes for a single frame (*Delete*) or the entire animation (*Clear*).

Make sure you set the current frame in the position needed to edit a particular keyframe!

7.1.3 Timeline navigation

An essential tool for your animation projects in Blender is the ability to navigate the Timeline. Once you learn how to move back and forward inside the Timeline Editor, it will become much easier to manage animations.

The first thing to do is identify how to set a current frame, which will help insert keyframes for properties.

In the 3D Viewport, you will find the current frame from your animation on your screen's top left. It appears next to the name of your active Collection. Using the Timeline Editor, you will also be able to see the current frame at the top right, and also set the start and end frames (Figure 7.8).

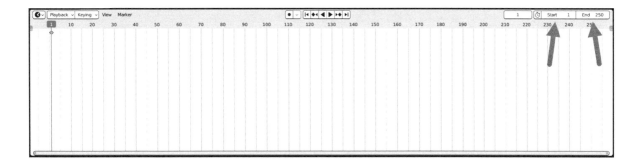

Figure 7.8 - *Timeline Editor*

A few shortcuts you will want to use for animation control:

– **SPACEBAR**: Play the animation.

– **LEFT ARROW**: Jump one frame backward.

– **RIGHT ARROW**: Jump one frame forward.

– **UP ARROW**: Jump to the next keyframe.

– **DOWN ARROW**: Jump to the previous keyframe.

– **SHIFT+LEFT ARROW**: Jump to the start frame.

– **SHIFT+RIGHT ARROW**: Jump to the end frame.

You can also navigate the Timeline using the playback head, which is the vertical blue line marking the current frame. Using the left mouse button, you can click and drag that line to change the current frame.

That same line appears in several other animation related editors, like the Graph Editor and the Dope sheet.

Tip: The shortcuts used at the Timeline Editor also works on all other animation related Editors.

7.2 Creating a simple animation

Now that we know how to create keyframes and navigate in the Timeline Editor, it is possible to create a simple animation. The purpose of the animation is to make an object move in the 3D Viewport. You can use any object as an example of the animation.

In our case, we can grab a text object that you can create using the SHIFT+A keys and choosing the Text option. To edit the text contents, go to Edit Mode with the text selected, and replace it as if you were in a text editor.

For the animation, we can use the following data:

– **Length**: 2 seconds

– **FPS**: 30

– **Start frame**: 1

– **End frame**: 60

Change most of the settings for this animation in the Timeline Editor. Only the FPS requires the Output tab at the Properties Editor to update from 24 to 30 the frame rate.

Tip: You can press the Home key to adjust the zoom of your Timeline editor after setting the Start and End frames.

Our animation subject starts on the left side of our 3D Viewport and move to the right. The animation uses location keyframes only. Select the object you want to animate and make sure frame 1 is your current frame (Figure 7.9).

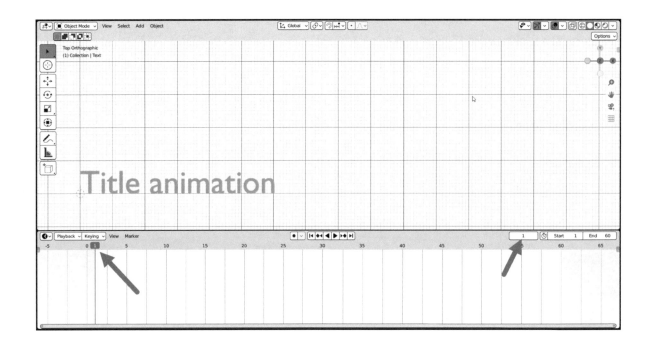

Figure 7.9 - Animation start

Press the I key and choose a location keyframe. You can also use the Sidebar or the Object tab in the Properties Editor to add keyframes. There you will right-click above the Location field and choose Insert Keyframes.

The Timeline Editor now displays a diamond-shaped icon for the selected object in frame 1 (Figure 7.10). Notice that the object name and active Collection will also turn to yellow, indicating a keyframe. Those names appear at the top left your 3D Viewport.

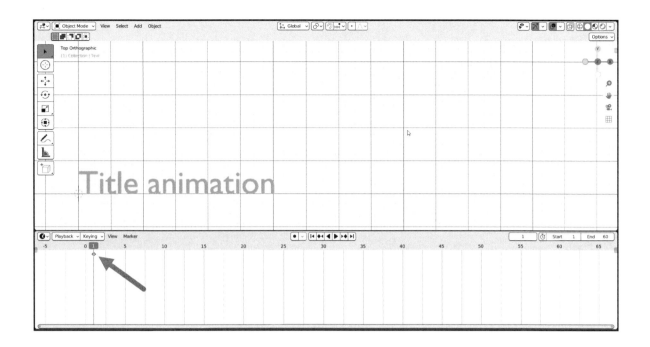

Figure 7.10 - *Timeline with keyframe*

Move the current frame to 60 and keep the text object selected. Press the G key and move your 3D object to the right. Once the 3D object is on the right side, press the I key, and choose location again. A new keyframe appears in the Timeline (Figure 7.11).

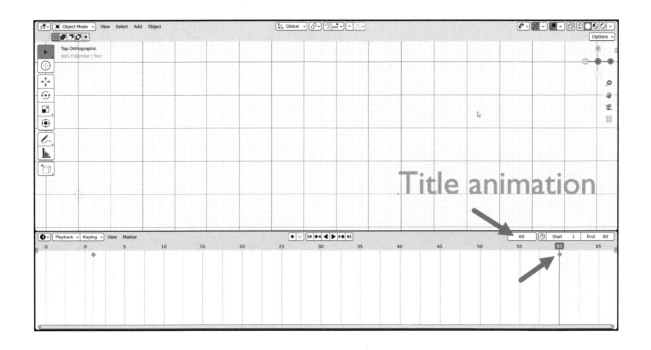

Figure 7.11 - Second keyframe

To start and preview animations, press the SPACEBAR key or the play button in the Timeline. That starts playing any animation you have in all Editors.

We can expand the animation, making the object stay still for one second and then going back to your screen's left side. First, add two seconds to the total length of our animation. In the Timeline Editor, change the End frame from 60 to 120.

Tip: *Use the mouse wheel to adjust the zoom and view all frames from 1 to 120. The Home key can also adjust the zoom of your Timeline Editor.*

To make your object stay still in animation, repeat the same keyframe. In our case, you can set the current frame to 90 and press the I key with the object selected. Do not make any changes to the object location. Choose the location keyframe type.

As an alternative method, you can also select the keyframe with a left-click at the Timeline Editor and press SHIFT+D. That duplicates your keyframe. Move it to position 90 and confirm with another left-click.

You will notice that from frames 60 to 90, a solid line appears connecting both keyframes in the Timeline (Figure 7.12).

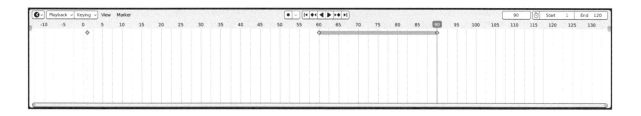

Figure 7.12 - Timeline with solid lines

That is a visual representation of two keyframes with no changes between properties. Since we didn't move the object, it has the same location value for both keyframes.

Go to frame 120 and move your object to the left side of your screen. Once there, press the I key and choose the location keyframe type again. Press the SPACEBAR key, and you will see the object starting in the left and moving to the right. After staying still for one second, it will go back to the left side.

303

Besides the solid line connecting two keyframes that shares the same data, you will also find other places displaying animation data color codes. In the Sidebar and Object tab properties with a:

– **Yellow background**: means an existing keyframe at the current frame

– **Green background**: Value created by interpolation between two keyframes

Using those color codes helps to identify when animation data exists in any property (Figure 7.13).

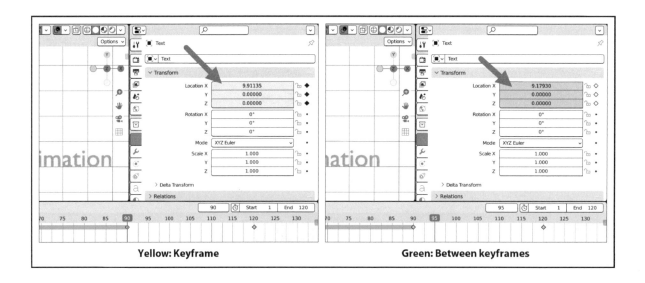

Figure 7.13 - Color codes

When you are in a frame where the selected object has a keyframe, your property displays a yellow background. For the intermediate frames where interpolation is occurring, the property background will be green.

7.3 Managing animation timing

You might want to make changes to the timing and speed of your animations in Blender after evaluating a project. To make such adjustments, you have to move keyframes back and forward for timing adjustments.

For instance, if you take the animation created in section 7.2, we can perform timing adjustments straight in the Timeline Editor. There you can select each keyframe, and with the G key moves them around.

By making two keyframes closer to each other, you make any animation faster. If you increase the distance between them, a slower animation is the outcome (Figure 7.14).

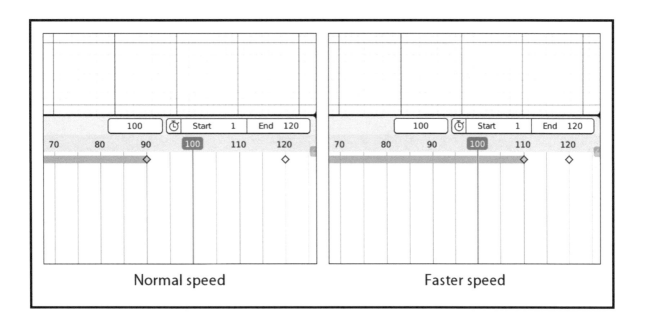

Figure 7.14 - *Timing adjustments for keyframes*

To manipulate keyframes in the Timeline or any other editor in Blender, use the same selection keys and transformations from 3D modeling projects.

If you want to adjust the entire animation timing, a scale transformation is the best choice. Press the A key to select all keyframes and use the S key to scale up or down animation as the whole (Figure 7.15).

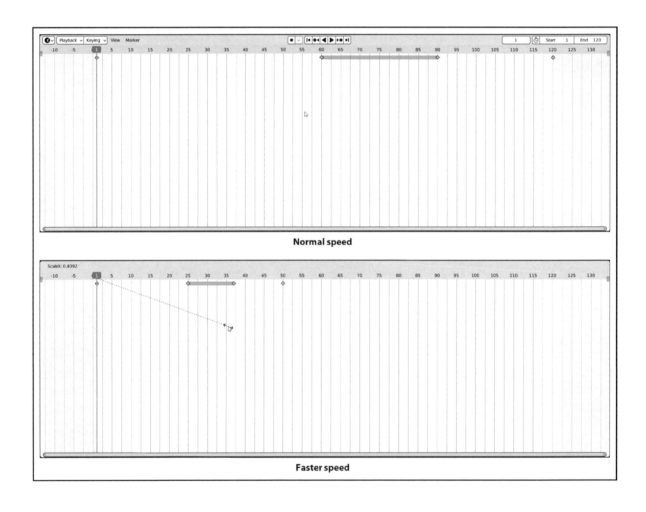

Figure 7.15 - *Timing the entire animation*

By using a scale transformation, you must be careful with the current frame. That frame works as the pivot point for the scale. To keep your animation starting in the same frame, make sure you set the current frame as the first one from your animation, before pressing the S key.

Using any other frame as the current frame during a scale might completely change your animation's Start and End frames.

Tip: You can also use the Snap at the Timeline Editor. Select a keyframe and press SHIFT+S to show options related to animation.

7.4 Controlling animation with curves

If you take a close look at the animation created in section 7.2, notice that it's not linear. The object gains speed in the beginning and slows down by the end of each period of animation. That type of motion for animations has the name of easing.

Any interpolation animation created in Blender uses easing for motion regardless of the property. To view and edit that type of animation data, we can use the Graph Editor, which shows a visual representation of all motion as curves (Figure 7.16).

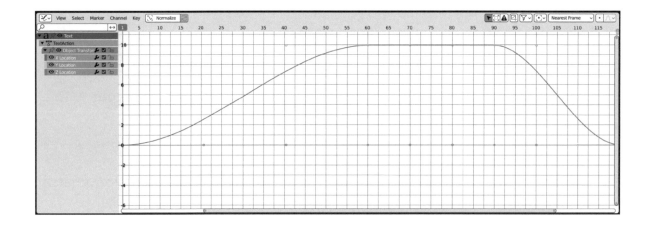

Figure 7.16 - Graph Editor

Change the Timeline Editor in the interface to a Graph Editor, using the Editor Type selector.

There you will see a lot more information about animations than what is available at the Timeline. For instance, you will be able to see individual animation channels on the left. Some controls to lock animations (padlock icon) and hide curves from the editor (checkbox icon).

The graphs display animation data using the horizontal axis for the frames and vertical axis for the property values.

Use the same zoom controls to adjust the viewing of your curves. With the Home key, you can fit all curves and keyframes in the current editor. If your keyboard doesn't have a Home key, use the **View → Frame All** menu.

The keyframes appear as small dots at the start and end of each curve (Figure 7.17).

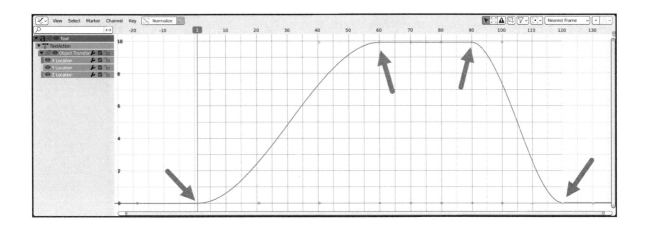

Figure 7.17 - *Keyframes in the Graph Editor*

If you select a keyframe and use the G key to move it around, you will see the curve structure adjusting to the new keyframe location. Besides changing keyframes, you will also see the control handlers (Figure 7.18).

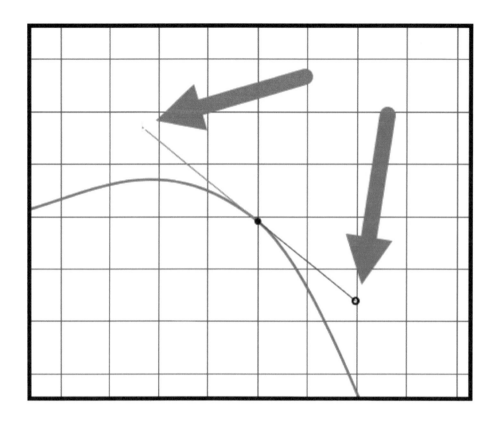

Figure 7.18 - *Control handlers*

By selecting the handlers, you can deform the curve and change the animation's speed and easing.

Another option to edit animation data inside the Graph Editor is with the Sidebar. With a keyframe selected, you can press the N key to open the Sidebar for the Graph Editor and change the values for that particular keyframe (Figure 7.19).

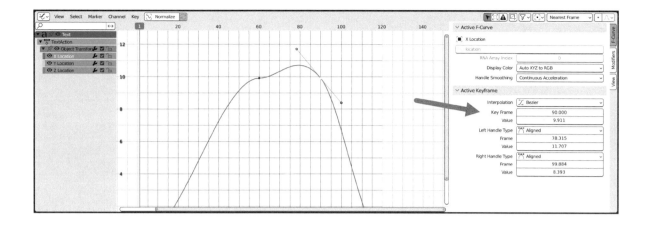

Figure 7.19 - Keyframe values

At the Key field, you can change the frame and also the value for the property that has a keyframe. It is an easy way to make changes to any keyframe.

To remove any easing from the animation, you can change the Interpolation Modes. In the Graph Editor, press the A key to select all keyframes and go to the **Key → Interpolation Mode** menu. There you will choose the **Linear** option.

That changes your curves to straight lines, which will turn the motion to a linear progression with no easing (Figure 7.20).

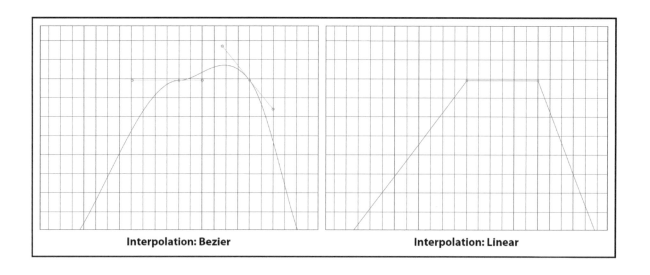

Figure 7.20 - *Linear motion*

Regarding animation, always use easing when you want to create natural movement, and for artificial motion, like machines, use the linear interpolation.

7.5 Hierarchies for animations

For animation projects that demand multiple objects interacting with each other, an option that can create hierarchical relations between 3D models will become useful. That tool allows an animator to create a movement based on a parenting relation between objects.

In Blender, you create hierarchies for animation using the CTRL+P keys to parenting objects. To make it easier to understand, we can name two objects in a hierarchy as parent and child:

- **Parent**: Object that can receive transformations and will replicate all of them to the children.

- **Child**: Object that inherits all transformations from the parent. If you rotate or move the parent, all children will also receive the same animation. However, any transformation applied to the child won't affect the parent.

For instance, if we have a 3D model like the one shown in Figure 7.21, we can make it work as a robotic arm. All we have to do is adjust the correct parenting relation between each object.

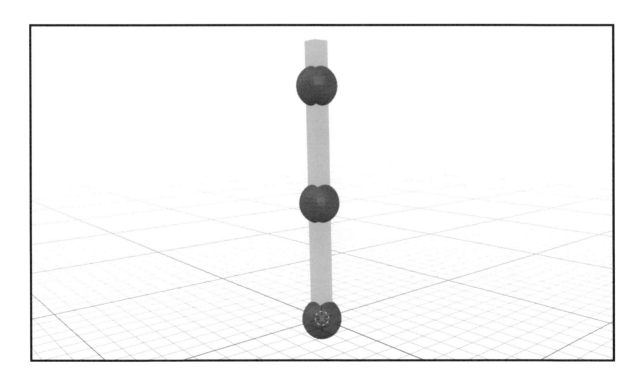

Figure 7.21 - *Objects for robotic arm*

For a robotic arm motion, use the object near the base as the main parent for all structures. To create a parenting relation, you must select at least two objects. The last object selected (*Active Object*) will always be the parent.

Starting with the top two objects, select the child, and while holding the SHIFT key, select the parent. Press the CTRL+P keys to create a parent and child relation (Figure 7.22).

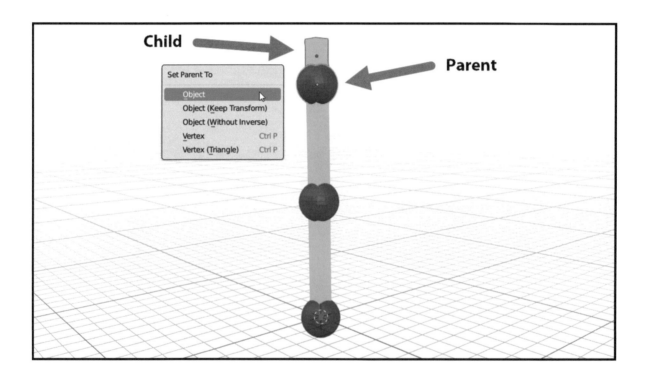

Figure 7.22 - Parenting selection

Suppose you make a mistake, press ALT+P to break the connection. How to verify the parenting? Simple, select the parent, and apply a rotation. You will see the child object following the same rotation from a parent.

314

All child objects follow transformations from their parents. Repeat the parenting process for the remaining parts of the model, according to Figure 7.23.

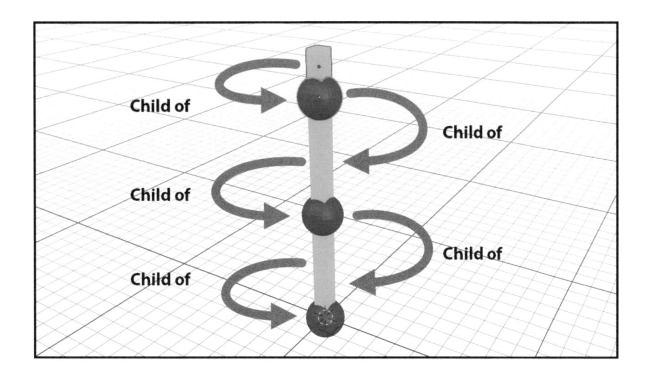

Figure 7.23 - Parenting structure

After you have the full model with parenting relations, an arm's animation becomes a lot easier. By selecting the base sphere of the object, you will move and rotate the entire arm. Select the spheres and apply individual rotations to create poses for the arm (Figure 7.24).

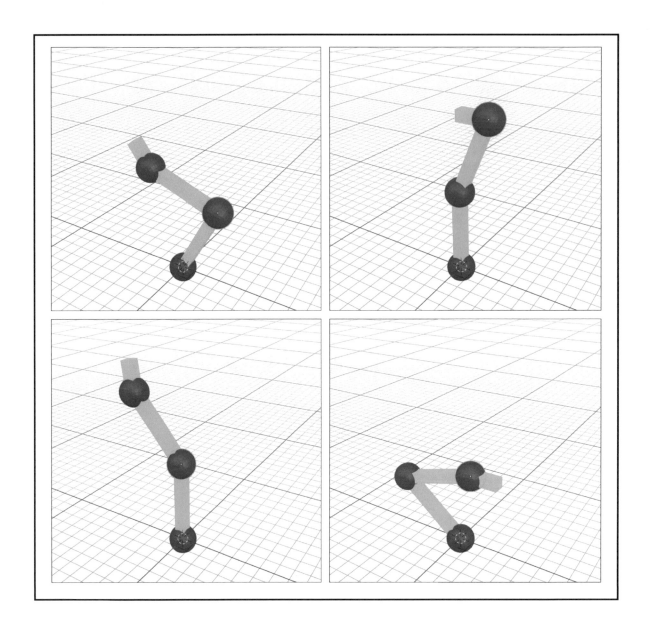

Figure 7.24 - *Arm positioning*

You can apply rotation keyframes to the spheres and make an animation with the arm. In those animations, you easily go back to the rest position (*Initial position*) by clearing all rotations—Press ALT+R to reset a rotation with a sphere selected.

Use the ALT key with any transformation shortcut to return the object property to their original value. The same option is also available from the **Object** → **Clear** menu.

Tip: *You can also create an object like the one shown in Figure 7.21 using only cubes and spheres. Apply transformations and move them to stay with the same formation from the image.*

7.6 Constraints for animations

In animation projects, you might want to use a special type of tool that will help to create motion with interactions between objects. The constraints can add certain rules to animated objects, making a few types of projects a lot easier.

You will find them in the Properties Editor in the Object Constraint tab (Figure 7.25).

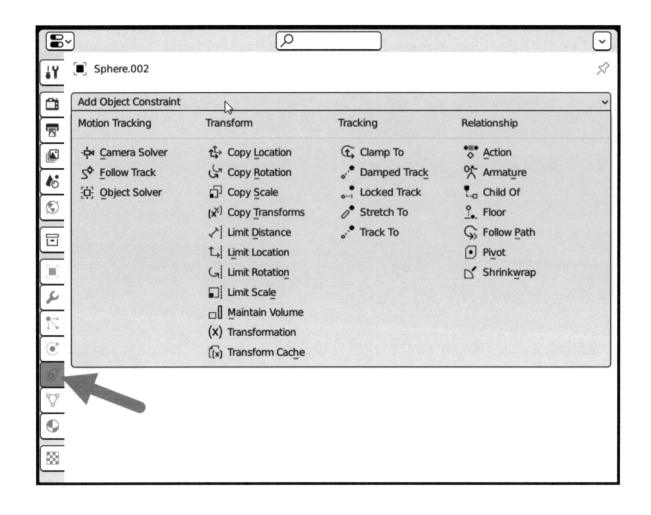

Figure 7.25 - Object constraint

After adding a constraint to an object, you will have unique options for each constraint type. The panel works like options from modifiers, where you can manage and reorder constraints applied to any selected object.

Among constraint types available, you will find:

– Copy Location, Copy Rotation, and Copy Scale: **Makes the selected object using the same transformation data from the target object.**

– **Limit Location, Limit Rotation, and Limit Scale**: Makes the object chosen to receive a limit for each transformation based on a target object.

– **Child of**: You can create parenting relations that can receive keyframes.

A key component of all constraints is the Influence option. With the influence, it is possible to set how each constraint affects object motion. An influence of 1.000 means it has a 100% impact on the motion. By dropping that value to zero, it is possible to "turn off" a constraint.

You can easily add keyframes to the influence settings, by placing the mouse cursor above the influence field and pressing the I key. That opens a world of possible animations we can create using constraints.

7.6.1 Making an arm grab an object

An easy example of what we can do with animation constraints is making an arm grab an object. To make our example simple, we can use the same structure created in section 7.5 with the same parenting relations.

For the animation, we will use the structure, a sphere, and three empties to mark key locations for animation (Figure 7.26).

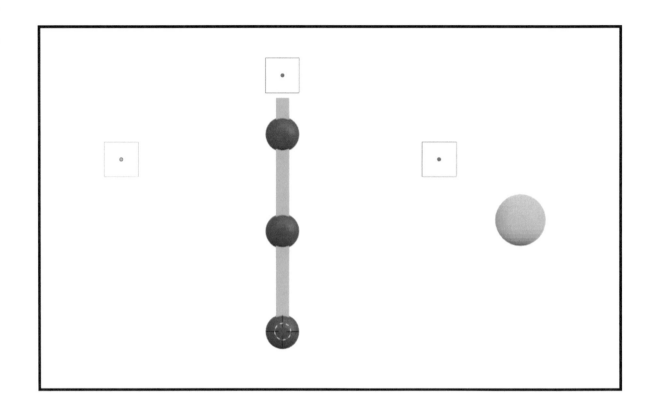

Figure 7.26 - *Scene for animation*

The objective is to make our structure grab the sphere and release it on the opposite side. It is a simple animation, which would require a lot of work to create without constraints.

Before we start, set all objects relations using the parenting tool. The empty close to our arm's tip must be a child of the object at the top, named "hand." Select the empty first and then the "hand." Press CTRL+P to create a parenting relation.

Info: You will see a dashed line connecting the Empty and "hand" once they have a parenting relation.

Using the F2 key to rename all empties with the following names:

– **Empty near the sphere**: firstEmpty

– **Empty near the "hand"**: armEmpty

– **Empty on the right**: endEmpty

Our animation will have 120 frames and an FPS of 30. Press the R key, to apply rotations and bend the arm:

– **From frame 1 to 30**: Rotate the arm close to the "firstEmpty."

– **From frame 31 to 90**: Rotate the arm to the other side, close to the "endEmpty."

– **From frame 91 to 120**: Rotate the arm away from the "endEmpty."

The animation occurs only in the sphere objects, and to clear your motion between frames 90 and 120, you can press ALT+R at frame 120.

By pressing the SPACEBAR key, you will see the arm moving in the 3D Viewport, but the sphere remains in the same location.

Now, select the sphere object and apply three "Copy Location" constraints. In each constraint, choose as the target object one of the empties. Change the influence of the constraints with the "endEmpty" and "armEmpty" to zero (Figure 7.27).

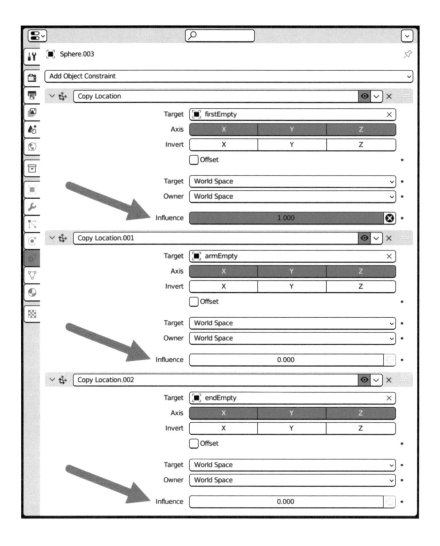

Figure 7.27 - *Constraints for sphere*

Make sure your current frame is 1 and apply a keyframe to all influences. You can either right-click on each property and choose "Insert keyframe..." or place the mouse cursor above each influence and press the I key (Figure 7.28).

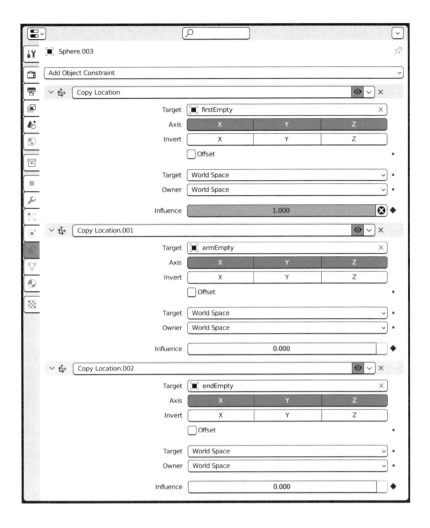

Figure 7.28 - Keyframes for constraints

Remember that you can add keyframes to any property in Blender using the same procedure. Place the mouse cursor above a property and press the I key.

Go to frame 30 and insert keyframes to all of the influences again. In frame 31, when your arm gets closer to the sphere, change the influences. Change the influence to zero for the constraint with "firstEmpty" as a target and one for the "arm-Empty" constraint (Figure 7.29).

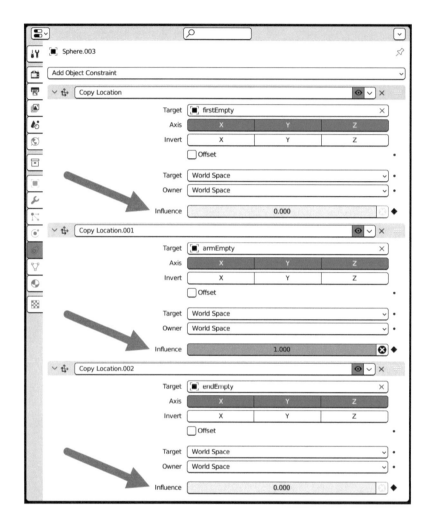

Figure 7.29 - Influences for constraints

Apply keyframes to all constraint influences again. By previewing your animation, you see that the arm will "grab" the sphere in frame 31. From that point forward, the sphere follows any movement of the arm.

Go to frame 90 and apply keyframes to all influences in the three constraints. In frame 91, change the constraint's influence with the "armEmpty" as the target to zero and the "endEmpty" to one. Apply keyframes to all of the constraint influences (Figure 7.30).

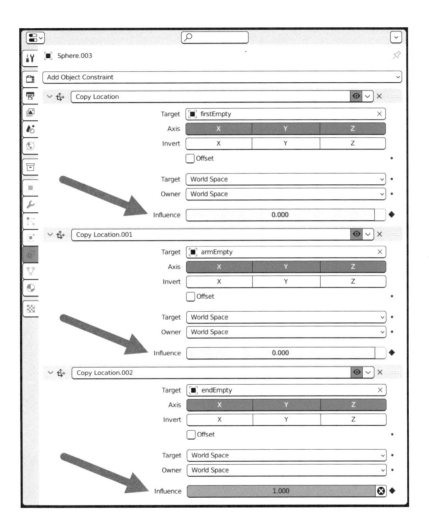

Figure 7.30 - Last keyframes

If you preview your animation, the arm moves until it grabs the sphere at frame 31. Our structure bends and rotates towards the opposite side, carrying the sphere. In the end, it releases the object on the left side of your 3D Viewport, at frame 91.

That is just one example of what we can do with constraints for animations.

What is next?

The creation of animations is a time-consuming task in any software, and you will find that Blender shares that same aspect of animation production. For each idea or project, requiring animations, you need some time to create and set up all motion and timing right.

A great way to learn and develop animations skills is to make quick and small projects related to motion graphics. It can be a simple plane with a texture with a logo, which enters the screen with additional text.

Or you can make fly through animations using only camera motion. Regardless of the project type, you should try to create a small animations portfolio to develop your skills. Use Eevee for rendering to cut on render times for animation production.

The next chapter helps you with additional information regarding animation production like editing content, adding titles, and making objects follow predefined paths.

Chapter 8 - Animation rendering and composition

To finish our Beginners Guide for Blender, you will learn how to improve and work with additional animation production options. Like including a "missing" feature to the Blender camera, which is a target.

Using a particular type of constraint and an Empty, you can create a target for any camera that helps with framing. You can make a camera follow any object moving around in a scene using that target.

Another cool feature involves 2D curves for animations, which can help with a type of animation called "Turntable." In those animations, your objects stay still, and the camera will "fly" in a circle around the target — a great option to show 3D models using animation.

Here is a list of what you will learn in this chapter:

– How to make a camera always look to the same object with a Track To constraint

– Make objects follow a path in animation

– Creating animation loops in the Graph Editor

– Render and export video for animation

– Use the Video Sequencer Editor

– Edit, Cut, and compose animations with the Sequencer

– Add backgrounds for animations in the Sequencer

– Add titles for animations using the Sequencer

8.1 Following an object with the camera

Camera framing is an important aspect of any project in Blender for both still images and animations. You might want to use a feature that makes a camera follow an object's motion for animations. That will be useful on several occasions where you have an important subject in animations.

To make your camera follow any object in a scene, use a constraint called *Track To*. Since that constraint is important for animations, it features multiple ways to assign into a 3D model:

- **Using the Constraint tab at the Properties editor**: Select the camera and add the Track To option.

- **Go to the Object → Track → Track To Constraint menu**: Select the camera first and the target object last. Use the menu option to add the constraint.

Both options add a constraint to the camera object that you can edit at the constraint tab (Figure 8.1).

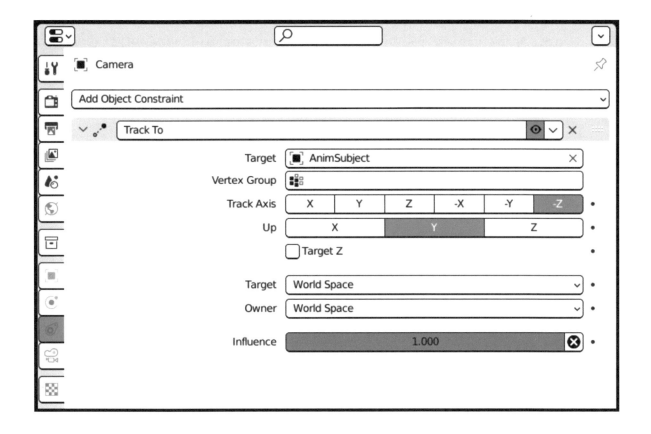

Figure 8.1 - *Track To Constratint*

At the options, you must specify a target object that your camera must follow, and also the axis used for tracking:

– **To**: Use the -Z option to make your camera look to the object.

– **Up**: Here, you have to use the Y option to align the camera Y-axis with the world Y-axis. Don't change this option unless you want to rotate the camera.

Now you have the camera following all movements made by the target object. If you use the **Object → Track → Track To Constraint** menu, the target object will be set automatically. For that, you must select the target first and the camera last.

8.1.1 Making an object following a path

Besides making the camera follow an object for animation, we can also use a curve path to help with complex trajectories. If you try to move objects in animation using lots of curves and turns, using a curve object might improve any motion.

Using a curve object in Blender, we can make any 3D model use that curve as a path. You can create curve objects using the SHIFT+A keys and go to the Curve group (Figure 8.2).

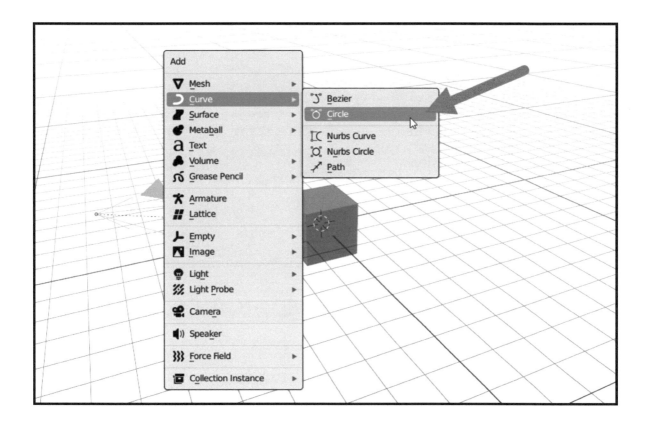

Figure 8.2 - *Curve objects*

From the curve object list, you will see two types of objects:

– **Bezier**: A curve that will feature points control handlers.

– **Circle**: A curve that also has points and control handlers, but already in a circle shape.

Using the Circle option creates a circular shape that can work as a path for animation. If you make the camera follow that circle and use a Track To constraint, you will create an animation called "Turntable." In that animation, a camera flies around an object in a circular trajectory.

Assuming you have a 3D model already at the scene. You can follow these steps to create a turntable animation:

1. Create the Circle from the Curve group.

2. Adjust the scale and Z coordinate of your curve with the S and G keys.

3. Select the camera first, and holding the SHIFT key, add the circle to the selection.

4. Press the CTRL+P keys and choose "Follow Path."

5. Select the camera only and got o the **Object** → **Clear** → **Origin** menu. That will make the camera origin to align with the circle.

6. Select the camera, and holding the SHIFT key, add the object you want to stay at the center of your circle to the selection.

7. Go to the **Object** → **Track** → **Track To Constraint** menu.

If you press the SPACEBAR, you will see the camera following the circle as a path for the animation.

Tip: *Use an Empty as the target for your camera. That way you will have more flexibility to move the focus point for your animation.*

By default, your follow path animation always start with 100 frames as length. It uses 100 frames regardless of your settings for Start and End frames. You can change that by selecting the Circle and opening the Object Data tab. There you will find a field called Path Animation (Figure 8.3).

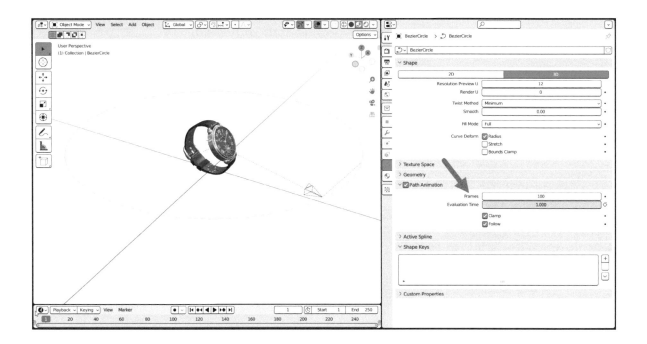

Figure 8.3 - *Path Animation*

Change the Frames option to the amount you want to use for the animation. If you are using the default animation length with an End in frame 250, you can repeat the same value in the Frame field. It will use the entire range of your Timeline.

To break the Follow Path animation, you can select the object following the curve and press ALT+P. Choose the "Clear Parent" option, and the object stops following the curve.

Tip: *Be careful not to create a Circle from the Mesh group instead of the Curve. The Circle from the Mesh group doesn't support the Follow Path animation.*

8.2 Creating animation loops

Animations in Blender always work in a linear direction, where you define a Start and End frames for them. During playback, the animation begins and ends based on those two frames. However, using a special feature of the Graph Editor, it is possible to make any motion to loop forever or with a defined number of repetitions.

To make an animation loop, you must create the motion first and prepare it to use a loop. For instance, if you want to make an object go back and forward forever, you should work in a way that your last frame uses the same property location value as the first frame.

That way, your motion always ends at the starting point. Ready to begin again!

An excellent way to make animations that shares the first and last positions with the same property values is to add all keyframes before applying any motion. In Figure 8.4, we have an object that we can animate by making it scale up and down.

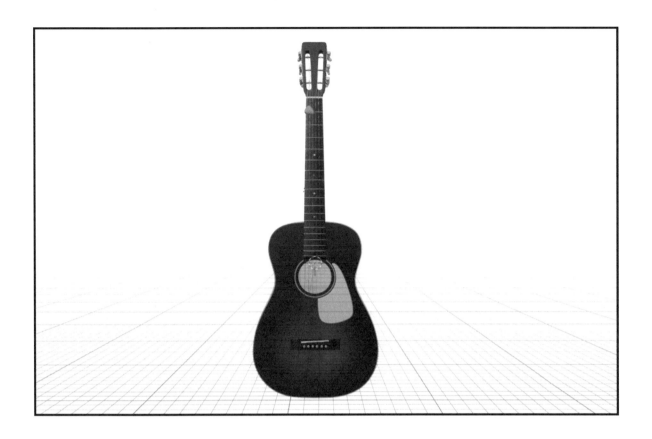

Figure 8.4 - Object for animation

The animation will have 1.5 seconds using 30 FPS, which means we need 45 frames. Here is the animation breakdown:

– **Frame 1**: Object will have a scale factor of 1

– **Frame 22**: Object will have a scale factor of 1.5

– **Frame 45**: Object will have a scale factor of 1

Select the object and add a scale keyframe for frames 1, 22, and 45. Since you didn't apply any scale transformation, all keyframes share a scale factor of 1. As an alternative, you can use a SHIFT+D after inserting the first keyframe at the Timeline Editor.

Go to frame 22 and apply a scale to the object with a factor of 1.5 by:

1. Pressing the S key

2. Type 1.5

3. Press RETURN to confirm

4. Press I, and add a Scale keyframe to update animation data with the new scale value

Part of the trick of using animation loops is that you should skip the last frame. At the animation settings, make the Start and End frames as 1 and 44. Why not 45 for the End frame?

The reason to use 44 is simple: you want to avoid having two consecutive frames using a scale factor of 1. If you use frame 45 as the End, you will have frame 45, and 1 played in sequence. It will create a brief stop for your animation and break the fluidness of motion.

8.2.1 Using modifiers in the Graph Editor

With the animation ready, we can create the loop by using modifiers in the Graph Editor. Those are different types of modifiers and don't have any relation to modeling modifiers. Open the Graph Editor and press the N key to view the Sidebar (Figure 8.5).

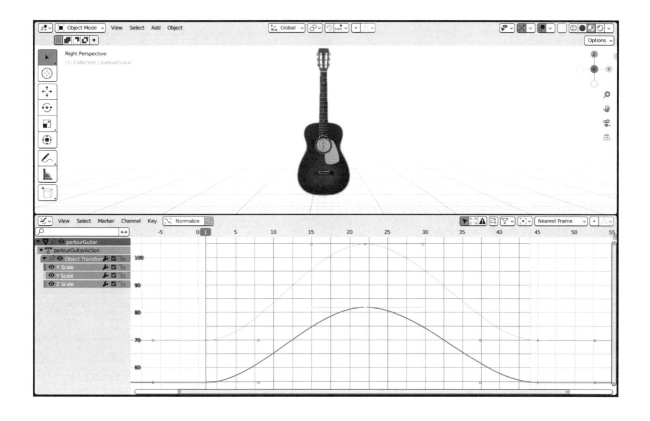

Figure 8.5 - Graph Editor

When we talk about a Sidebar in Blender, you probably think about the 3D Viewport Editor. But, some other Editors also have a Sidebar like:

– Graph Editor

– Dope Sheet

– Shader Editor

– Video Sequence Editor

– Image Editor

For this animation exercise, we have to open a Sidebar for the Graph Editor. Place the mouse cursor above your Graph Editor when pressing the N key to open that Sidebar.

At the Sidebar, open the Modifiers tab and add a Cycles modifier to the curves. That creates an animation loop for your selected curves. You will immediately see the difference with the curve visualization extending before and after the original shape (Figure 8.6).

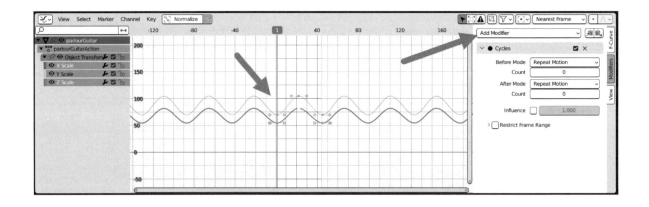

Figure 8.6 - Animation loop

It is possible to control certain aspects of your loop at the Cycles modifier options. At the Before and After options, you can control the number of repetitions.

Using zero for both, you get the animation repeating forever, or you can pick a number of repetitions to limit your loop. Below you can also restrict the Start and End frames used for the loop.

8.3 Organizing projects in scenes

Each project you work in Blender has something called Scene that you can later reference or use for rendering. The scene selector is at the top right of your interface and always start with the default "scene" (Figure 8.7).

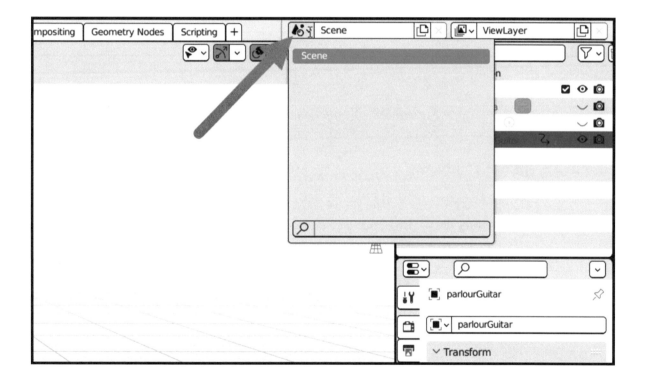

Figure 8.7 - *Scene selector*

There you can change the current scene and create new ones based on a few options. If you click at the button to the right of your scene name, you will see the types of scenes you can create (Figure 8.8).

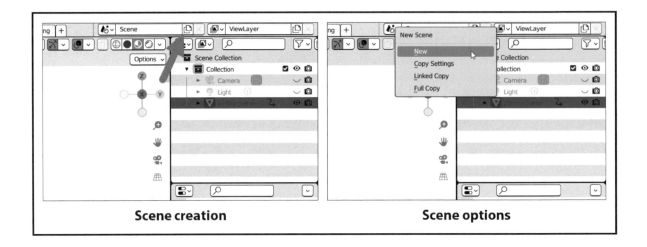

Figure 8.8 - Scene creation options

From the options you have:

– **New**: A completely new and independent scene that won't have any objects. An empty new scene.

– **Copy Settings**: An empty new scene that will use some of the settings used from the current scene.

– **Linked copy**: A copy of your current scene that has links to all objects and settings. If you have to create animations with the same objects but using unique types of motion, you can use it.

– **Full copy**: A copy of your current scene with all models and settings but no links with the original objects.

Besides working as a way to organize large projects in Blender, you can also use scenes to render projects in any specific order. If you use the Video Sequencer Editor, it will be possible to instance a full scene for animation editing.

In animation projects, it is common to have multiple takes for the same motion. You can use different scenes to work with shots featuring unique effects and play them in a row at the Video Sequence Editor.

The Video Sequence Editor works like a non-linear video editor inside Blender, and it is possible to insert full scenes in a timeline for video composition. For instance, you can have an introductory scene that has a title animation. Then a second scene with all main elements of a project.

8.4 Rendering animation

After you have a full animation with cameras and all the objects ready, it is time to start rendering the project. Unlike a still image where you can manage and view the final result at the Output window, an animation with dozens, hundreds, or thousands of frames requires a dedicated folder to either save a video or image sequence.

Before starting an animation rendering, you have to pick a folder for the project in the Output tab (Figure 8.9).

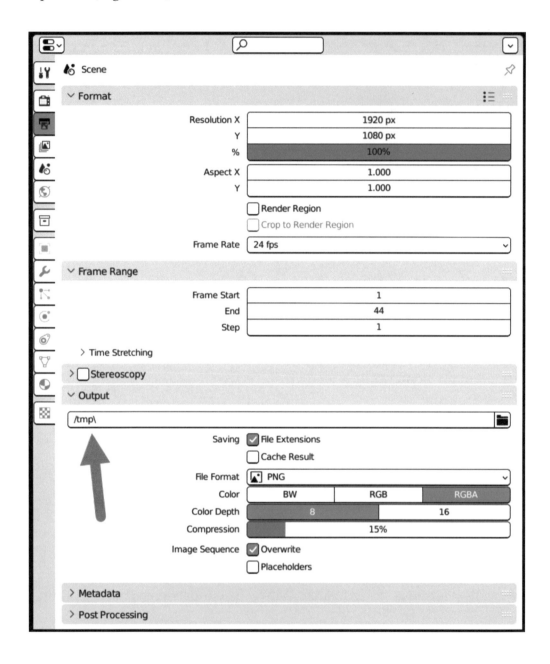

Figure 8.9 - *Output folder*

There you can set a folder in your computer or local network, that will store all frames or video from an animation.

Once you have the output folder selected, it is time to make an important choice regarding your rendering. You can save your animation result as a video file or image sequence:

- **Video file**: You can render the animation in formats like MP4, MKV, or OGG

- **Image sequence**: The animation will appear as a sequence of individual image files like PNG or JPG.

Having your animation rendered as a video file might be convenient for quick visualization. But if you want to have a flexible workflow and avoid the need for rendering everything again, you should use an image sequence.

The most significant benefit of working with an image sequence is that you can keep a lossless version of all your animation frames. By choosing the PNG image format, you can later generate a video file and include titles and effects.

Another benefit of using image sequences is that you can easily stop and resume a rendering process with no data loss. For instance, by rendering animation with 5000 frames, you can interrupt the process at frame 750. You can later resume the rendering by setting your animation to start from frame 751, which will keep your previous progress.

8.4.1 Rendering as a video file

In case you want to use a video file for the animation output, you have to choose the proper option in the "File Format" field of the Output tab. There you will see three main options for the Movie output:

– AVI JPEG

– AVI Raw

– FFmpeg video

Unless you have a very specific reason, avoid using the first two options. If you want to use modern video containers for your animation like MP4, choose the FFmpeg video option. With that option, a new panel opens at the bottom of your output settings with a name of Encoding (Figure 8.10).

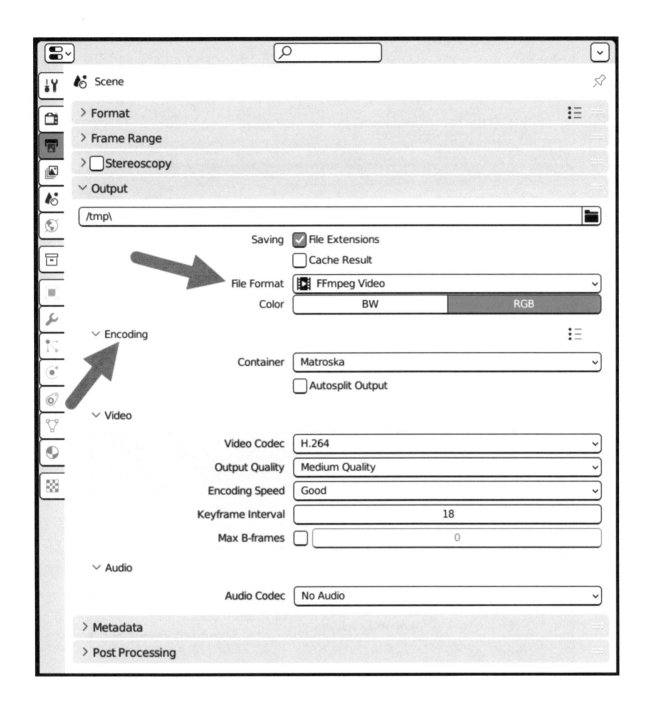

Figure 8.10 - *Video output*

At the Encoding options, you will choose several options to create an MP4 file or several other formats. For a quick set up in video rendering, you can use existing presets available at the location shown in Figure 8.11.

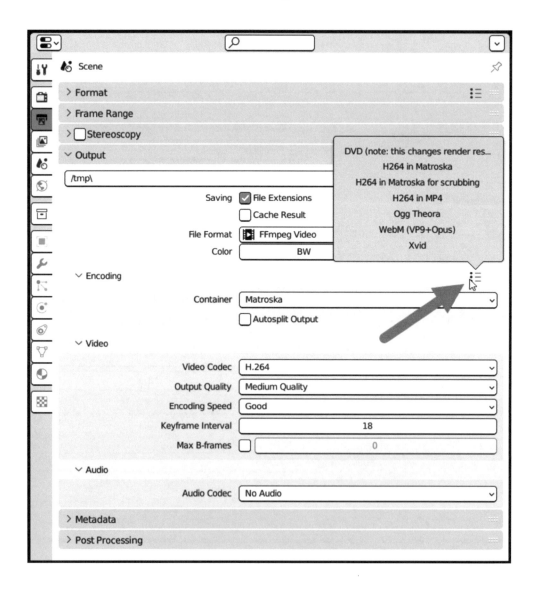

Figure 8.11 - *Video presets*

One of the presets has "h264 in MP4" that already has all the options to create such a file. If you want to render animations for platforms such as YouTube, an MP4 file with h264 is a great choice.

You might want to change a few details about the video to tweak the quality. For instance, change the Output quality from "Medium quality" to "High quality" to get much better quality for animation rendering. Those settings will improve aspects like video bitrate.

That keeps your video file with the highest possible quality and will most likely generate a large file. In the audio field, you will notice that it shows the option "No audio." Because our animation's frames from the 3D Viewport doesn't feature any audio, you should keep the option as "No audio" (Figure 8.12).

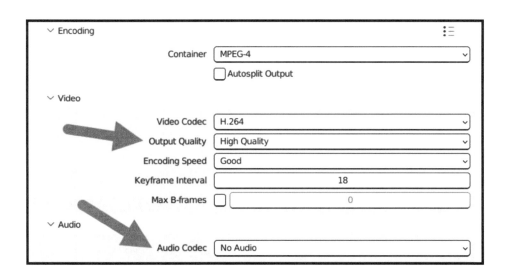

Figure 8.12 - *Video encoding*

You can add audio for any animation later in the Video Sequencer Editor and use those settings to control both format and quality for any audio data.

After choosing where and how to save your animations, it is time to start rendering. You can either press CTRL+F12 or use the **Render → Render Animation** menu. The rendering of animation will most likely take a long time, and you should prepare the computer to stay processing the project for a while.

For projects using Cycles for rendering, processing might require a couple of hours or days to complete. That depends on a combination of how complex your project is and the available hardware. You can have an idea about how long it will take by making a quick calculation.

If one frame takes on average 1 minute to render and the full length of your animation has 2400 frames, it will take 2400 minutes (1-minute x 2400) to finish. That will roughly give 40 hours of rendering — almost two days of processing the animation.

To reduce that time, you can do a few things:

– Use lower values for sampling and activating the Denoising feature in Cycles;

– Upgrade your hardware! Getting a better GPU (*Graphics processing unit*) might dramatically reduce rendering times. A few options include high-end cards like the RTX family from NVIDIA, which will give you an option to use OptiX Denoising. A better CPU with multiple cores might also give a speed boost.

– Optimize your scene and remove any visual effects or features slowing down the render. Add those same effects later in post-processing.

Since the computer hardware market constantly changes in short periods, I recommend checking the Blender Open Data:

– https://opendata.blender.org/

There you will find a list with currently available computer hardware and their performance for rendering. That is by far the best source of information regarding computer hardware for rendering in Blender.

Once the rendering process comes to an end, you will see the file created in the Output folder (Figure 8.13).

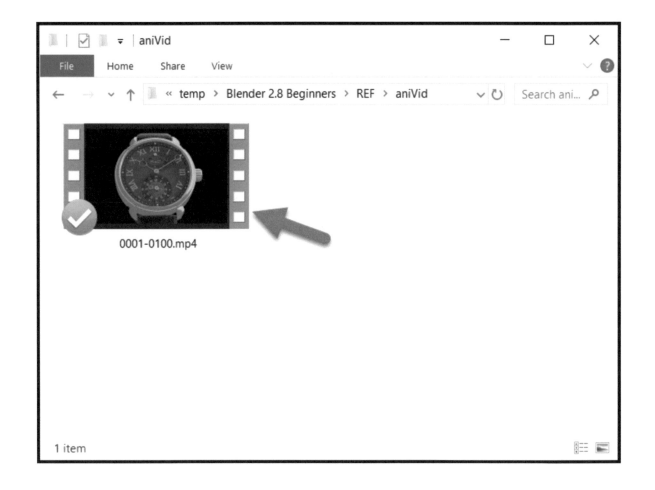

Figure 8.13 - *Video saved in the Output folder*

The same applies to an image sequence, but instead of a single file, you will see one image file for each frame.

Tip: A benefit of rendering animations as image sequences is that you can start over the process in case of a problem. For instance, if your computer crashes after rendering frame 1000 from 2400, you can come back and start from frame 1001. In a video file, you would have to start from the beginning.

8.5 Editing and exporting video

The rendering of animation to either a video file or image sequence is the starting point of a process that results in your project's final version. You will most likely use multiple scenes for the animation, effects, and titles. It is possible to edit and add those features in Blender without the need for any external editors.

One of the Editors from Blender can handle and manipulate video files and works like a non-linear video editor. Using the Video Sequencer Editor, or VSE, you can build large animations by manipulating separate pieces of projects like video shots, effects, and more.

We mentioned the VSE when describing Scenes' use, and it is now time to explore that Editor.

To use the VSE, you can use any available space from the interface or open a dedicated WorkSpace for video editing. The WorkSpace is the best choice because it already offers all the options to edit and process video comfortably.

From the WorkSpace selector, you can choose **Video Editing** → **Video Editing** to rearrange the interface with all required spaces to work with video editing (Figure 8.14).

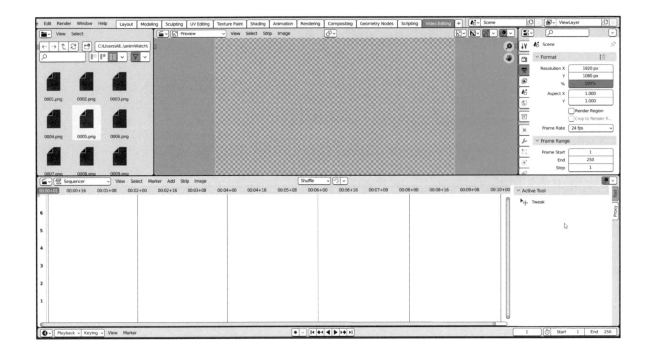

Figure 8.14 - *Video Editing WorkSpace*

At the bottom, you will see the Video Sequencer Editor with all the channels that can receive tracks such as video, audio, and image sequences. Each channel works like a layer, where you can stack media on top of each other. At the top, you have another Video Sequencer Editor, but with the Preview mode active. That shows a preview of all your media.

In the top right, you have the rendering output settings and a file browser on the left.

You can add content to the editor using the Add menu and choose from video files (Movie), Audio files (Sound), or Image/Sequence (Figure 8.15).

354

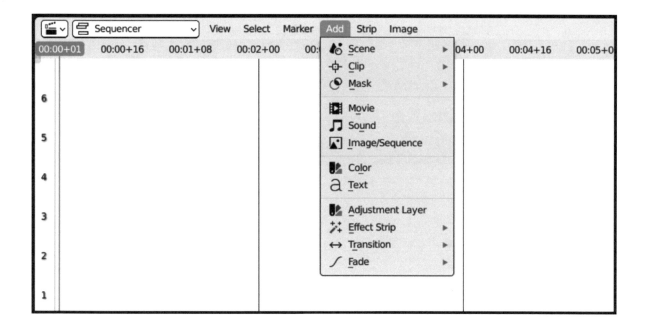

Figure 8.15 - *Add menu*

For instance, we can select the Image/Sequence option and select all files from a sequence with the A key. They will appear in the sequencer as a block of content called Strip (Figure 8.16).

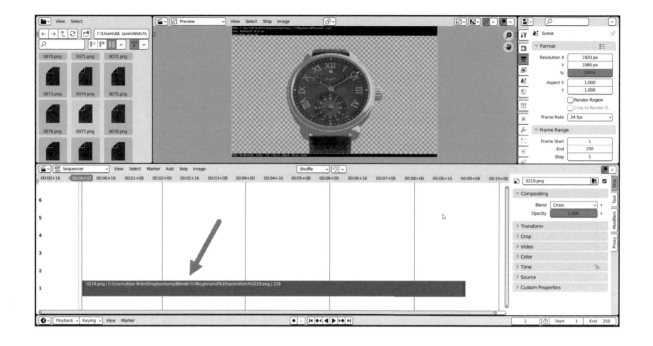

Figure 8.16 - Image sequence as a track

To edit and change aspects of any Strip, you can use the same shortcuts applied in 3D modeling tasks. The most used shortcut to manipulate Strips is the G key. Select any Strip and press the G key to move it back and forward in time.

At the borders of the strip, you also find a vertical marker at the beginning and end. You can click to select those markers and using the G key contract or expand the Strip.

If you enabled the transparent option for rendering PNG files as an image sequence, you would be able to compose it with a background easily. Since each channel works as a layer, Strips at the bottom always appear in the back of a composition. Placing a still image at the bottom of your stack makes it appear in the back (Figure 8.17).

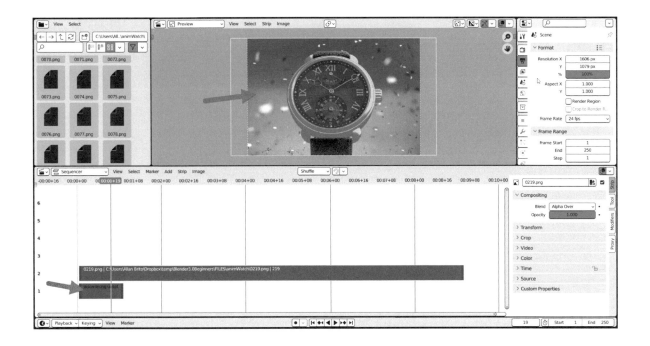

Figure 8.17 - *Image in the back*

To ensure you can see a composition using transparent PNG sequences, make sure you have the Alpha Over option at your Sequencer's Sidebar. By default, a Strip starts with the Alpha Over enabled. Only with that option active, you see transparency applied to Strips (Figure 8.18).

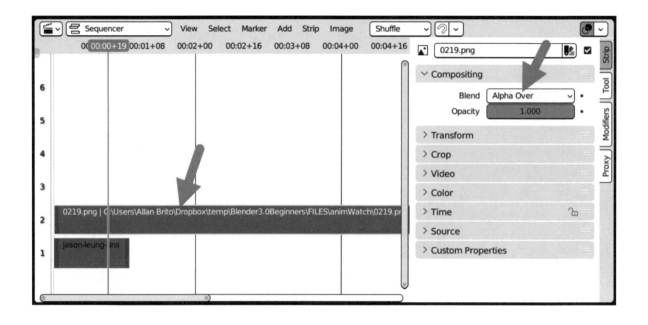

Figure 8.18 - *Alpha Over effect*

At the bottom, you also have an Opacity control a Strip transparency. That is useful in case you need a watermark in a video project.

Tip: You can add keyframes to any property in the Sequencer Sidebar.

8.5.1 Editing video

With the Video Sequencer Editor, you have most of the tools and options from a traditional video editor. For instance, you can cut Strips to remove or reorder parts of your animation. To cut a video, you use the K key with a Strip selected (Figure 8.19).

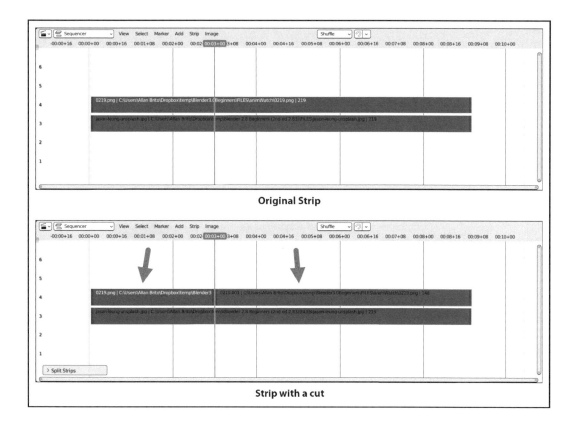

Figure 8.19 - *Cutting a strip*

Place the animation cursor at the frame you wish to use to cut and press the K key. After you cut a Strip, it will be possible to select each part and:

– Reorder your remaining parts.

– Erase parts of a Strip.

– Duplicate and copy parts of a Strip. You can duplicate Strips with a SHIFT+D.

You can't join two different Strips. Instead, we can make something called a MetaStrip. That is a composed Strip made from several parts. To create a MetaStrip: select multiple Strips and press the CTRL+G keys (Figure 8.20).

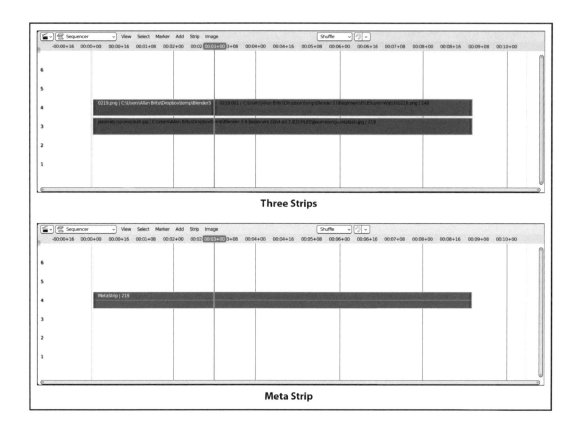

Figure 8.20 - *MetaStrip*

If you select a MetaStrip and press the TAB key, you will be able to edit that group's contents. You can break a MetaStrip with the CTRL+ALT+G keys.

8.5.2 Exporting video

Once you add any content to the Video Sequencer Editor, any rendering from Blender will output your video sequence contents even if you go back to the 3D Viewport and add more content to the original animation. By pressing CTRL+F12, you only see the results of your video editing project.

The reason for that is because of a setting from the Post Processing field at the Render tab. There you will find the "Sequencer" option enabled by default.

Unless you disable the Sequencer option, Blender will always output contents from the video sequencer instead of 3D data from your 3D Viewport. If you want to go back to the 3D Scene to change animation aspects, make sure you disable the Sequence option to render it again (Figure 8.21).

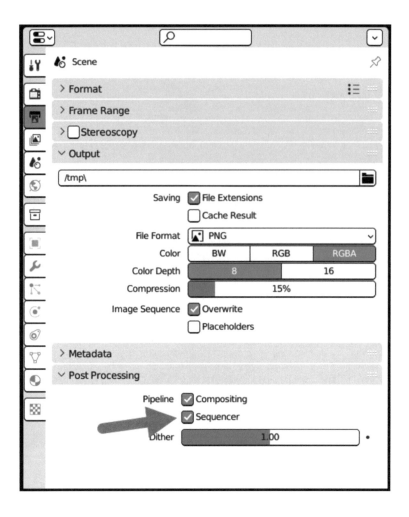

Figure 8.21 - Sequencer option

In case you have to edit an existing render, use a different Blender project to edit and cut the animation.

8.5.3 Converting images sequences to video

By adding an image sequence to the Video Sequence Editor, you can convert that to a video file like an MP4. Add the image files as a Strip and change the output settings to use FFmpeg. Pick the settings you need for an MP4 file and start rendering it again.

That is the moment where you can convert an image sequence to a video file, and also add sounds or music. From the Add menu in the Sequencer, you can include Sound strips to the project.

Rendering a video from an image sequence will be much faster than generating all the content from 3D objects. Since you already processed the 3D content, it will be a matter of converting all the effects and images to video.

8.6 Adding titles and text

Most animation projects need some titles in the video to display information before or after the content. That could help you to add credits to the video or a simple title for a project.

To add text to any video in the Sequencer, use the Add menu, and choose the Text option (Figure 8.22).

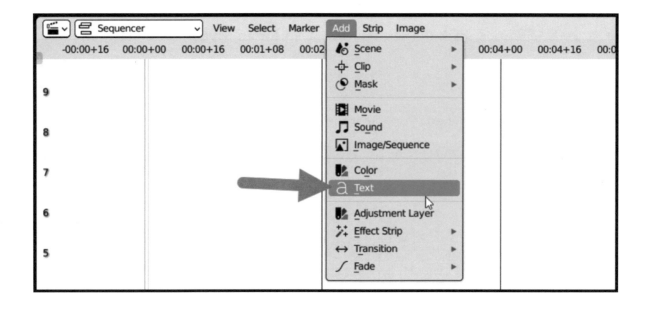

Figure 8.22 - *Text for video*

The text will appear as a separate Strip to edit their contents by selecting the Strip and using the Sidebar. You will find options to change details like the font and the text contents (Figure 8.23).

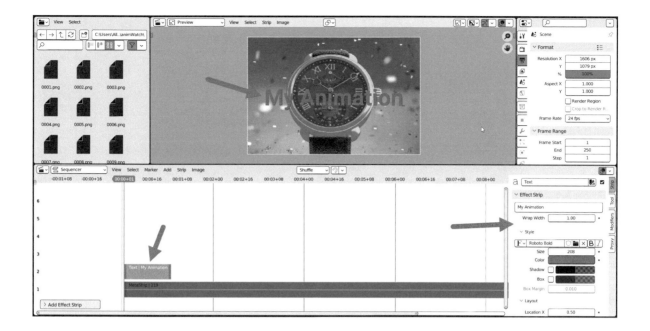

Figure 8.23 - Text details

Add as many text Strips you need for your project, and once you have all the required information for a project, press the CTRL+F12 keys to start rendering your video. Remember that your text should be at your sequencer's top channels if you want it appearing on top of any Strips.

What is next?

You know, have a solid base to create lots of different types of projects in Blender from 3D modeling, rendering, and animation. The next step now is to get some ideas for projects regarding visualization and animation for practicing.

In the first projects, you will probably find some speed bumps and problems. But with a little patience and the help of our book, you will find most solutions.

Don't miss the opportunity to develop even more your skills with Blender. Only with personal projects will you take the next step and start migrating to more complex projects with:

– Character animation

– Advanced rendering

– Visual FX

– Advertising creation

– Architectural visualization

– Product design

– Game Development

Blender can help you with all those projects, and all you need is to focus your projects on a particular subject. Then you will start acquiring experience in each one of those fields.

Manufactured by Amazon.ca
Bolton, ON

32292602R00201